HEINEMANN MODULAR MATHEMATICS

for

EDEXCEL AS AND A-LEVEL

Statistics 2

Greg Attwood   Gill Dyer   Gordon Skipworth

Heinemann

Edexcel

Success through qualifications

Heinemann Educational Publishers,
a division of Heinemann Publishers (Oxford) Ltd,
Halley Court, Jordan Hill, Oxford, OX2 8EJ

OXFORD   MELBOURNE   JOHANNESBURG   AUCKLAND
BLANTYRE   IBADAN   GABORONE   PORTSMOUTH NH (USA)
CHICAGO

First published 2000

02   01   10   9   8   7   6   5   4   3   2   1

ISBN 0 435 51083 5

Cover design by Gecko Limited.

Original design by Geoffrey Wadsley: additional design work by Jim Turner

Typeset and illustrated by Tech-Set Limited, Gateshead, Tyne and Wear

Printed in Great Britain by The Bath Press, Bath

Acknowledgements:

The publisher's and authors' thanks are due to the Edexcel for permission to
reproduce questions from past examination papers. These are marked with an [E].
    The answers have been provided by the authors and are not the responsibility
of the examining board.

About this book

This book is designed to provide you with the best preparation possible for your Edexcel S2 exam. The series authors are senior examiners and exam moderators themselves and have a good understanding of Edexcel's requirements.

Use this **new edition** to prepare for the new 6-unit specification. Use the first edition (*Heinemann Modular Mathematics for London AS and A-Level*) if you are preparing for the 4-module syllabus.

Finding your way around

To help to find your way around when you are studying and revising use the:

- **edge marks** (shown on the front page) – these help you to get to the right chapter quickly;
- **contents list** – this lists the headings that identify key syllabus ideas covered in the book so you can turn straight to them;
- **index** – if you need to find a topic the **bold** number shows where to find the main entry on a topic.

Remembering key ideas

We have provided clear explanations of the key ideas and techniques you need throughout the book. Key ideas you need to remember are listed in a **summary of key points** at the end of each chapter and marked like this in the chapters:

■ If X is a continuous random variable with p.d.f. $f(x)$

$$f(x) \geqslant 0 \; \forall \; x$$

Exercises and exam questions

In this book questions are carefully graded so they increase in difficulty and gradually bring you up to exam standard.

- **past exam questions** are marked with an [E];
- **review exercises** on pages 59 and 109 help you practise answering questions from several areas of mathematics at once, as in the real exam;
- **exam style practice paper** – this is designed to help you prepare for the exam itself;
- **answers** are included at the end of the book – use them to check your work.

Contents

3 Continuous distributions

4 Hypothesis tests

Basic mathematical techniques

There are four basic mathematical techniques that are prerequisites for S2. Binomial coefficients in connection with the binomial distribution and the evaluation of the exponential function are both dealt with in chapter 1 in the context in which they will be used. General notes on the differentiation and integration of polynomials are given below. More detailed information on these matters may be found in Book P1.

Differentiation of polynomials

Differentiation is a process for finding the rate at which one variable quantity changes with respect to another. For example, if y is a function of x, and y changes by a small amount, Δy, due to a small change, Δx, in x, then the differential (written as $\dfrac{dy}{dx}$ or $f'(x)$ in functional notation) is defined as the limit of $\dfrac{\Delta y}{\Delta x}$ as Δx approaches zero. This idea is illustrated below.

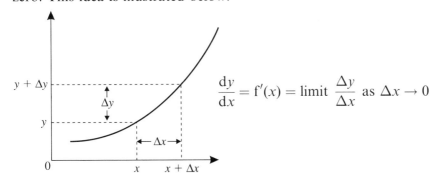

$$\frac{dy}{dx} = f'(x) = \text{limit } \frac{\Delta y}{\Delta x} \text{ as } \Delta x \to 0$$

A polynomial is an expression such as $y = 3x^2 + 2x + 4$, i.e. where y is given in integer powers of the variable x. Any other pair of letters may, of course, designate the variables. In the case of polynomials there is a general formula for finding $\dfrac{dy}{dx}$.

■ **When $y = kx^n$ where k is a constant:**

$$\frac{dy}{dx} = nkx^{n-1}$$

In simple terms you multiply by the index and then subtract one from it.

So if $y = 3x^4$ then $\dfrac{dy}{dx} = 4 \times 3x^{4-1} = 12x^3$.

This may be extended to the case where there are several terms by using the following:

- **When $y = u \pm v$ where u and v are functions of x:**
$$\frac{dy}{dx} = \frac{du}{dx} \pm \frac{dv}{dx}$$

That it to say, you differentiate each term independently.

Example 1

If $y = 3x^3 - 6x^2 + 4$ then $\dfrac{dy}{dx} = 3 \times 3x^{3-1} - 6 \times 2x^{2-1} = 9x^2 - 12x^1$

(Notice that $x^0 = 1$ so 4 may be written as $4x^0$ and the formula applied giving $4 \times 0x^{-1} = 0$.)

Example 2

If $y = 4x^4 + 2x^2 + 4x$ then $\dfrac{dy}{dx} = 16x^3 + 4x + 4x^{1-1}$
$$= 16x^3 + 4x + 4$$

Integration of polynomials

Integration is the reverse of differentiation.

An integral is denoted by the symbol $\int$. We write:

$$\int f(x)\,dx \qquad \text{meaning}$$

the integral of $f(x)$ with respect to x

Since integration is the reverse of differentiation, if you differentiate a function then integrate the result you arrive back at the original function.

So to integrate a polynomial you do the reverse of differentiating; that is to say, you add 1 to the index and divide by the (index + 1). This gives the general law:

- $\displaystyle\int x^n\,dx = \frac{x^{n+1}}{n+1} + c \quad (n \neq -1)$ **where c is an arbitrary constant.**

The arbitrary constant c arises because if $y = 3x^2 + c$ then $\dfrac{\mathrm{d}y}{\mathrm{d}x} = 6x$ whatever the value of c. Integrals of this sort are known as **indefinite integrals** because the constant c could take any value.

Example 3

$$\int (3x^2 + 4x + 6)\,\mathrm{d}x = \int (3x^2 + 4x + 6x^0)\,\mathrm{d}x$$

$$= \frac{3x^3}{3} + \frac{4x^2}{2} + \frac{6x^1}{1} + c$$

$$= x^3 + 2x^2 + 6x + c$$

Example 4

$$\int \tfrac{1}{2}(x^2 - 5x + 3)\,\mathrm{d}x = \int \tfrac{1}{2}(x^2 - 5x + 3x^0)\,\mathrm{d}x$$

$$= \tfrac{1}{2}\left[\frac{x^3}{3} - \frac{5x^2}{2} + \frac{3x}{1}\right] + c$$

Definite integrals

A second type of integral is known as a **definite integral**. Definite integration gives you the area between the curve or line and the x-axis.

For example:

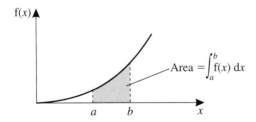

If you integrate between the limits a and b then you get the area of the shaded part of the diagram. With definite integration the notation is modified to show the limits between which the area is being calculated. You write the area shown above in general terms as:

$$\int_a^b \mathrm{f}(x)\,\mathrm{d}x$$

In order to evaluate such an integral, the integration is done first and then its value with $x = a$ is subtracted from its value when $x = b$. You do not have to worry about the constant c when integrating since it increases both of the values by the same amount. It changes the difference between them by $c - c = 0$.

Example 5

Find $\int_1^4 x^2 \, dx$.

$$\int_1^4 x^2 \, dx = \left[\frac{x^3}{3}\right]_1^4$$

$$= \left[\frac{4^3}{3}\right] - \left[\frac{1^3}{3}\right]$$

$$= \frac{64}{3} - \frac{1}{3}$$

$$= \frac{63}{3}$$

$$= 21$$

Example 6

Find $\int_1^3 (x^2 + 4x + 3) \, dx$.

$$\int_1^3 (x^2 + 4x + 3x^0) \, dx = \left[\frac{x^3}{3} + \frac{4x^2}{2} + \frac{3x}{1}\right]_1^3$$

$$= \left(\frac{3^3}{3} + \frac{4 \times 3^2}{2} + \frac{3 \times 3}{1}\right) - \left(\frac{1^3}{3} + \frac{4 \times 1^2}{2} + \frac{3 \times 1}{1}\right)$$

$$= (9 + 18 + 9) - (\tfrac{1}{3} + 2 + 3)$$

$$= 30\tfrac{2}{3}$$

Quadratic equations

The solution of a quadratic equation is needed in chapter 2. A reminder of the techniques for solving quadratic equations of the form $ax^2 + bx + c = 0$ is given below.

If $ax^2 + bx + c = 0$ then the solutions (or roots as they are called) of this quadratic equation can often be found by factorising $ax^2 + bx + c$.

Example 7
Solve the equation $2x^2 - x - 3 = 0$.

Solutions are given by

$$(x + 1)(2x - 3) = 0$$

So: $(x + 1) = 0 \quad$ or $\quad (2x - 3) = 0$

$$x = -1 \text{ or } +1\tfrac{1}{2}$$

Alternatively, the roots may be found using the formula

$$x = \frac{-b \pm \sqrt{(b^2 - 4ac)}}{2a}$$

Example 8
Solve the equation $3x^2 + 2x - 6 = 0$.

$$x = \frac{-2 \pm \sqrt{(2^2 - 4 \times 3 \times (-6))}}{2 \times 3}$$

$$= \frac{-2 \pm \sqrt{76}}{6}$$

$$= -1.79 \text{ or } +1.12$$

The binomial and Poisson distributions

1

1.1 Factorial notation

In Book S1 you saw that there are six arrangements of 2 red and 2 blue beads, namely:

RRBB	*BBRR*
RBRB	*BRBR*
RBBR	*BRRB*

To answer such a question in cases where the numbers are larger, you need a formula.

In a classroom there is a white board and a line of four holes for keeping the marker pens for use on the board. Usually four different coloured pens are in use: red (*R*), blue (*B*), black (*K*) and green(*G*). At the end of each lesson the pens are placed in the four holes. How many different *arrangements* are there for the pens.

Notice that the *order* is all important here as *RBKG* and *RBGK* are different arrangements. Sometimes a diagram can help in the visualization of the problem and aid in its solution. Imagine the four holes:

Hole 1	Hole 2	Hole 3	Hole 4
◯	◯	◯	◯

The first hole can be filled with any of the four coloured pens so there are 4 choices. The second hole could be filled with any of the remaining three colours so there are 3 choices for that hole and so on for the third and fourth holes.

Hole 1	Hole 2	Hole 3	Hole 4
◯	◯	◯	◯
4 choices	3 choices	2 choices	1 choice

Now suppose that the first hole was filled with *R*, there are still 3 possibilities for the second hole (*B, K* or *G*), so each of the four possibilities for the first hole gives rise to 3 choices for the second so the first two holes could be filled in

$$4 \times 3 = 12 \text{ ways.}$$

Extending this argument through all the holes, there are:

$$4 \times 3 \times 2 \times 1 = 24 \text{ arrangements of the pens.}$$

The multiplication $4 \times 3 \times 2 \times 1$ can be written as 4! and is called 4 **factorial**. This useful mathematical notation can be generalised as:

■ $n! = n(n - 1)(n - 2)\ldots 1$

When the black and red pens had to be replaced only blue and green ones were available, so there were now 2 blue pens and 2 green pens. How many arrangements are there now?

Let the two blue pens be B_1 and B_2 and the two green pens be G_1 and G_2. There are now 4 *different* pens B_1, B_2, G_1 and G_2, and 4! = 24 different arrangements. The arrangements are all listed below:

$B_1B_2G_1G_2$ $B_1G_1B_2G_2$ $B_1G_1G_2B_2$ $G_1G_2B_1B_2$ $G_1B_1G_2B_2$ $G_1B_1B_2G_2$

$B_1B_2G_2G_1$ $B_1G_2B_2G_1$ $B_1G_2G_1B_2$ $G_2G_1B_1B_2$ $G_2B_1G_1B_2$ $G_2B_1B_2G_1$

$B_2B_1G_1G_2$ $B_2G_1B_1G_2$ $B_2G_1G_2B_1$ $G_1G_2B_2B_1$ $G_1B_2G_2B_1$ $G_1B_2B_1G_2$

$B_2B_1G_2G_1$ $B_2G_2B_1G_1$ $B_2G_2G_1B_1$ $G_2G_1B_2B_1$ $G_2B_2G_1B_1$ $G_2B_2B_1G_1$

In reality of course there is no difference between the pens of the same colour so the subscripts can be removed. Notice that if the subscripts 1 and 2 are removed from the Gs then the top two rows are identical and so are the bottom two rows. So the total number of arrangements is reduced to

$$\frac{4!}{2} = 12$$

If the subscripts are then removed from the Bs then all four rows are identical and there are:

$$\frac{4!}{2 \times 2} = 6 \text{ arrangements.}$$

If the pens were then changed to 1 green and 3 blue pens we could group the arrangements into batches of 3! = 6. For example, one batch would be:

$GB_1B_2B_3$ $GB_1B_3B_2$ $GB_2B_3B_1$ $GB_2B_1B_3$ $GB_3B_1B_2$ $GB_3B_2B_1$

When the subscripts on the Bs are removed we are left with $\dfrac{4!}{3!1!} = 4$ arrangements, where the 3! is for the 3 Bs and the 1! for the G.

This important idea can be generalised so that if there are k different types of objects with n_1, n_2, n_3, $\ldots n_k$ of each type then the number of arrangements of all the objects is

$$\frac{(n_1 + n_2 + n_3 + \ldots n_k)!}{n_1! n_2! n_3! \ldots n_k!}$$

For example, with 6 pens consisting of $3B$, $2G$ and $1R$ the number of arrangements would be

$$\frac{6!}{3!2!1!} = \frac{6 \times 5 \times 4}{2} = 60$$

Example 1
A child has 4 yellow and 6 black identically shaped wooden bricks. The bricks are assembled into a vertical tower one brick deep. Find the number of different patterns of the bricks that can be formed.

Ten bricks with 4 Y and 6 B can be arranged in

$$\frac{10!}{4!6!} = \frac{10.9.8.7}{4.3.2.1} = 210 \text{ ways}$$

Example 2
In my pocket I have three £1 coins, two 50p coins and four 10p coins. I randomly select 3 coins to give my daughter her pocket money. Find the probability that the value of the coins is:

(a) £2.50   (b) £1.60   (c) 30p

(a) £2.50 must be made up of three coins, two one pound coins and one 50p coin. The number of arrangements is therefore

$$\frac{3!}{2!1!}$$

and the probability is given by

P(£1) $\times$ P(£1|£1 is already drawn) $\times$ P(50p|two £1 already drawn)
$\times$ no. of arrangements

$$= \frac{3}{9} \times \frac{2}{8} \times \frac{2}{7} \times \frac{3!}{2!1!} = \frac{1}{14}$$

(b) £1.60 must come from £1, 50p and 10p.

$$\text{probability} = \tfrac{3}{9} \times \tfrac{2}{8} \times \tfrac{4}{7} \times 3! = \tfrac{2}{7}$$

Notice that the 3! could be written as $\dfrac{3!}{1!1!1!}$, where the 1!s occur because there is simply one coin of each value.

(c) 30p comes from 10p, 10p and 10p.

$$\text{probability} = \tfrac{4}{9} \times \tfrac{3}{8} \times \tfrac{2}{7} \times 1 = \tfrac{1}{21}$$

Notice that the 1 could be written as $\dfrac{3!}{3!}$ since all three coins have the same value.

Exercise 1A

1 A play group has a large number of identical shaped coloured bricks. The children like to place the bricks in a straight line on the floor. Find the number of arrangements for the following sets of bricks.

(a) 3 red and 2 blue   (b) 8 red and 5 blue

(c) 4 red and 3 blue   (d) 2 red and 4 blue

(e) 7 red and 8 blue   (f) 6 red and 6 blue

(g) 10 red and 7 blue   (h) 1 red and 8 blue

2 A bag contains 6 red, 5 green and 9 yellow beads. Five beads are selected from the bag without replacement. Find the probability that they are:

(a) all yellow

(b) 3 red and 2 green

(c) 1 red and 4 yellow

If only three beads are selected

(d) find the probability of selecting one of each colour.

3 Repeat question 2 but this time selecting the beads with replacement.

1.2 The binomial theorem

Before the next distribution is introduced a small detour into pure mathematics is required to consider the expansion of expressions of the form $(p+q)^n$.

The expansion:

$$(p+q)^2 = p^2 + 2pq + q^2$$

should be familiar to you and you should be able to multiply this by $(p+q)$ to obtain:

$$(p+q)^3 = p^3 + 3p^2q + 3pq^2 + q^3$$

Clearly to keep multiplying in this way is very laborious and a better way of obtaining these **binomial expansions** is needed.

Consider the expansion:

$$(p+q)^3 = (p+q)(p+q)(p+q) = p^3 + 3p^2q + 3pq^2 + q^3$$
$$\quad\quad\quad A \quad\quad B \quad\quad C$$

Notice that each term of the expansion on the right is 'cubic'. This is because to work out $(p+q)^3$ you need to pick a term from bracket A, a term from bracket B and a term from bracket C so that eventually all possible arrangements are considered. [You might like to think how many arrangements there are. Remember two terms, p and q, to the power 3 gives 8 arrangements.] Your final expansion should consist of all *types* of cubic terms. These can be simply and systematically written down by starting with $p^3 q^0$ and then reducing the power of p and raising the power of q until $p^0 q^3$ is reached.

Remembering that this expansion generates *all possible arrangements* the final step is to find the coefficients of each term. For example, the $p^2 q$ term could arise as these arrangements – pqp or qpp or ppq – that is in three ways. As on page 8, this calculation could be written as:

$$\frac{3!}{2!\,1!} = 3$$

In the same way, you should now be able to write down any binomial expansion. For example, consider $(p+q)^5$.

The first stage is to write down the terms:

$$p^5 \quad p^4 q \quad p^3 q^2 \quad p^2 q^3 \quad pq^4 \quad q^5$$

Now the term $p^4 q$ could arise in:

$$\frac{5!}{4!\,1!} = 5 \text{ ways} \qquad (\text{as could } pq^4)$$

and the term $p^3 q^2$ could arise in:

$$\frac{5!}{3!\,2!} = 10 \text{ ways} \qquad (\text{as could } p^2 q^3)$$

So:

$$(p+q)^5 = p^5 + 5p^4 q + 10p^3 q^2 + 10p^2 q^3 + 5pq^4 + q^5$$

Notice that $1 + 5 + 10 + 10 + 5 + 1 = 32 = 2^5$ so all possible arrangements of p and q are included.

A general term for this expansion can be written as:

$$\frac{5!}{r!(5-r)!} p^r q^{(5-r)} \qquad r = 0, 1, \ldots 5.$$

The coefficient is sometimes written $\binom{5}{r}$ (or $5Cr$ on some calculators) and can be referred to as the number of combinations of r objects from 5, but a detailed knowledge of combinations is not required for S2.

Example 3

Find the term in the expansion of $(p+q)^{12}$ with p^7.

The required term will be of the form Kp^7q^5.
The coefficient will be:

$$\frac{12!}{7!\,5!} = 792$$

So the term is $792p^7q^5$.

Exercise 1B

1   Find the binomial expansion of $(p+q)^4$.

2   Find the binomial expansion of $(p+q)^6$.

3   In the expansion of $(p+q)^{10}$ find the terms in (a) p^3, (b) p^6, (c) p^8.

4   In the expansion of $(p+q)^{12}$ find the terms in (a) p^4, (b) p^8, (c) p^{10}.

5   Part of the expansion of $(p+q)^{15}$ is:

$$\ldots Ap^{13}q^x + Bp^{12}q^y + Cp^{11}q^z \ldots$$

Find the values of A, B, C, x, y and z.

6   Part of the expansion of $(p+q)^{13}$ is:

$$\ldots Ap^x q^{10} + Bp^y q^9 + Cp^z q^8 \ldots$$

Find the values of A, B, C, x, y and z.

7   Find the coefficient of the term p^7q^{13} in the expansion of $(p+q)^{20}$.

8   The term $Ap^{15}q^x$ arises in the expansion of $(p+q)^{20}$. Find the values of A and x.

9   Find the values of the following terms in the expansion of $(\frac{1}{3}+\frac{2}{3})^{10}$:

(a) $\binom{10}{7}(\frac{1}{3})^7(\frac{2}{3})^3$ (b) $\binom{10}{5}(\frac{1}{3})^5(\frac{2}{3})^5$ (c) $\binom{10}{6}(\frac{1}{3})^6(\frac{2}{3})^4$.

10 Find the values of A, B, C, x, y and z and evaluate the following terms in the expansion of $(\frac{1}{4}+\frac{3}{4})^8$:

(a) $A(\frac{1}{4})^5(\frac{3}{4})^x$ (b) $B(\frac{1}{4})^3(\frac{3}{4})^y$ (c) $C(\frac{1}{4})^z(\frac{3}{4})^2$.

1.3 Binomial distribution

A fair cubical die is rolled four times and the random variable X represents the number of sixes obtained. What can be said about the probability distribution of X?

Notice that there are four **trials** and each trial consists of rolling the die once. Each trial has only *two* **outcomes**: if a six is obtained then the outcome is a **success** whereas *any other* outcome is a **failure**. It is also reasonable to assume that the *trials are* **independent** since the outcome of the first trial does not affect the second or subsequent trials. Since the same die is used in each trial it is reasonable to assume that the **probability of a six** (i.e. success) **at each trial is constant** and as the die is fair the probability is equal to $\frac{1}{6}$.

If a success is represented by s and a failure by f, then the sequence *ssss* occurs with probability

$$\frac{1}{6} \times \frac{1}{6} \times \frac{1}{6} \times \frac{1}{6}$$

or

$$P(X = 4) = \left(\tfrac{1}{6}\right)^4$$

and the sequence *ffff* occurs with probability

$$\frac{5}{6} \times \frac{5}{6} \times \frac{5}{6} \times \frac{5}{6}$$

or

$$P(X = 0) = \left(\tfrac{5}{6}\right)^4$$

Notice that because the trials are independent you can multiply to find the probability of success on the 1st trial *and* 2nd trial *and* 3rd trial *and* 4th trial.

Consider now the situation where there are two successes and two failures. The sequence *ssff* occurs with probability

$$\frac{1}{6} \times \frac{1}{6} \times \frac{5}{6} \times \frac{5}{6}$$

but the event $\{X = 2\}$ includes all possible sequences of two s and two f. The number of possible arrangements in situations like this is given by:

$$\frac{4!}{2!\,2!} \qquad \text{or} \qquad \binom{4}{2} = 6$$

So:

$$P(X = 2) = 6 \times \left(\tfrac{1}{6}\right)^2 \times \left(\tfrac{5}{6}\right)^2$$

In a similar way you can see that:

$$P(X = 1) = \binom{4}{1} \tfrac{1}{6} \times \tfrac{5}{6} \times \tfrac{5}{6} \times \tfrac{5}{6}$$

$$= 4 \times \tfrac{1}{6} \times \left(\tfrac{5}{6}\right)^3$$

and $\qquad P(X = 3) = 4 \times \left(\tfrac{1}{6}\right)^3 \left(\tfrac{5}{6}\right)$

So the distribution of X is:

x:	4	3	2	1	0
$P(X = x)$:	$(\frac{1}{6})^4$	$4(\frac{1}{6})^3(\frac{5}{6})$	$6(\frac{1}{6})^2(\frac{5}{6})^2$	$4(\frac{1}{6})(\frac{5}{6})^3$	$(\frac{5}{6})^4$

Since X is a probability distribution then:

$$\sum_{x=0}^{4} P(X = x) = 1$$

and this could be verified but if you look at the binomial expansion of $(p + q)^4$:

$$(p + q)^4 = p^4 + 4p^3q + 6p^2q^2 + 4pq^3 + q^4$$

you can see that the probabilities in the distribution of X are simply terms in a binomial expansion with $p = \frac{1}{6}$ and $q = \frac{5}{6}$. It is then easy to see that:

$$(\tfrac{1}{6} + \tfrac{5}{6})^4 = 1^4 = 1$$

It is *this* relationship between the *probabilities* and the *binomial expansion* that gives rise to the term **binomial distribution** to describe this important discrete distribution.

It is important that you know the conditions under which a binomial distribution may provide a good model. These are summarised as follows:

Conditions for a binomial distribution:
- There must be a **fixed number** (n) of trials.
- The trials must be **independent**.
- The trials have only **two outcomes**: success or failure.
- The **probability of success** (p) is **constant** for each trial.

If these conditions are satisfied then the random variable X representing the number of successes in the n trials has a **binomial distribution** and the **probability function** is:

$$P(X = r) = \binom{n}{r}p^r(1 - p)^{n-r} \qquad r = 0, 1, 2, \ldots, n$$

For convenience $(1 - p)$ is sometimes written as q, i.e. $q = (1 - p)$ or $p + q = 1$. Thus $P(X = r)$ can be written as

$$P(X = r) = \binom{n}{r}p^r q^{n-r} \qquad r = 0, 1, 2, \ldots, n$$

That is, each probability is a term in the expansion of $(p + q)^n$.

The binomial distribution is a very important discrete probability distribution and there are many areas where it can be applied. In order to use it in a particular situation you need to ensure that the above conditions are satisfied and find values for n and p. The binomial distribution is actually a whole family of distributions, each member being determined by the particular values of n and p. Notice that n and p are sometimes referred to as the **parameters** of the binomial distribution. If the random variable X has a binomial distribution with parameters n and p this can be written as $X \sim \mathrm{B}(n,p)$.

Example 4

Only 75% of sunflower seeds from a particular supplier produce flowers when planted. If 10 of the seeds are planted find the probability of obtaining 8 or more flowers.

Let the random variable X represent the number of seeds that produce a flower. Then model X with a binomial distribution so that $X \sim \mathrm{B}(10, 0.75)$

$$\mathrm{P}(X \geqslant 8) = \binom{10}{8}(0.75)^8(0.25)^2 + \binom{10}{9}(0.75)^9(0.25) + \binom{10}{10}(0.75)^{10}$$

$$= 45(0.75)^8(0.25)^2 + 10(0.75)^9(0.25) + (0.75)^{10}$$

$$= 0.28156\ldots + 0.1877\ldots + 0.05631\ldots$$

$$= 0.52559\ldots$$

$$= 0.5256 \ (4 \text{ d.p.})$$

There are cumulative probability tables for the binomial distribution and these can sometimes be used to find approximate (4 d.p.) answers to problems. The Edexcel tables are given for $X \sim \mathrm{B}(n,p)$ for certain values of index n and p and give the cumulative probabilities $\mathrm{P}(X \leqslant r)$ for most values of r. So if $X \sim \mathrm{B}(10, 0.3)$ then from tables $\mathrm{P}(X \leqslant 6) = 0.9894$ or if $X \sim \mathrm{B}(5, 0.15)$ then $\mathrm{P}(X \leqslant 3) = 0.9978$. You could also use the tables to answer example 4 above. Define the random variable Y as the number of seeds that do *not* produce flowers then $Y \sim \mathrm{B}(10, 0.25)$ and the problem is equivalent to finding $\mathrm{P}(Y \leqslant 2)$. From tables this value is 0.5256 which agrees with the calculations above to 4 decimal places.

Although the tables give cumulative probabilities they can be used to find individual probabilities as well. Suppose $X \sim \mathrm{B}(20, 0.35)$ and you wish to find $\mathrm{P}(X = 9)$. This can be achieved as follows:

$$\mathrm{P}(X = 9) = \mathrm{P}(X \leqslant 9) - \mathrm{P}(X \leqslant 8)$$

$$= 0.8782 - 0.7624$$

$$= 0.1158$$

Of course individual probabilities can be calculated quite easily from the probability function so in this case:

$$\mathrm{P}(X = 9) = \binom{20}{9}(0.35)^9(0.65)^{11}$$

$$= 0.11584\ldots$$

$$= 0.1158 \ (4 \text{ d.p.})$$

but sometimes the tables are more convenient and save time.

As previously mentioned, a binomial distribution can be used to model a wide variety of situations. The random variable needs to be carefully defined to ensure that the conditions for a binomial apply. Consider using the binomial distribution to model the behaviour of woodlice. An apparatus is set up in the shape of a letter 'T', as shown in the diagram:

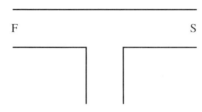

A substance that is attractive to woodlice is placed at one end of the apparatus near exit S. A woodlouse is released into the apparatus and the exit (F or S) from which it emerges is noted. If 20 different woodlice are used one at a time then the behaviour of the woodlice can be regarded as independent. It may be necessary to take some precautions in case, for example, the woodlice leave a trail behind them which a later woodlouse could follow.

If you assume that the woodlouse exits only via one of the two marked routes then S and F will provide you with your success and failure: a success will be when the woodlouse appears at exit S and a failure will be when it appears at F. What is the probability (p) of the woodlouse going towards the attracting substance? Does this depend upon the sex, species or size of the woodlouse? Is it a constant?

If the substance really is an attractor then p will be greater than $\frac{1}{2}$ but if the reactions of the woodlouse to it are fairly neutral then you might expect the value of p to be close to $\frac{1}{2}$. Some big assumptions about the value of p will have to be made before a binomial distribution can be used but a value of $p = 0.5$ is probably a good starting point for a preliminary model.

If you define the random variable W to be the number of woodlice which leave at exit S then B(20, 0.5) might provide a reasonable model for W. If it turns out that this model provides a reasonable fit then this would have important implications about the attractiveness of the substance to the woodlice.

Example 5
Explain whether or not a binomial distribution can be used to model the following situations. In cases where it can be used, give a definition of the random variable and suggest suitable values for the parameters n and p.

(a) The number of throws of a die until a six is obtained.
(b) The number of girls in a family of 4 children.
(c) The number of red balls drawn when 3 balls are drawn from an urn which contains 15 white and 5 red balls.

(a) A binomial distribution requires a fixed number of trials, n. The number of times the die is thrown can not be fixed in this experiment and so a binomial distribution is of no use.

(b) There is a fixed number of children in the family, so $n = 4$ and the 'trials' are 'children'. The trials can probably be assumed to be independent as if the first child is a girl, the gender of the other children should not be affected by this (identical twins could cause a problem though). There are only two possibilities for the outcomes of the trials and these can be defined in this example as success (a girl) and failure (a boy). It is probably reasonable to assume that p, the probability of a girl, is constant but what should that value be? An obvious solution is to use $p = 0.5$ but you could refer to national statistics which will give you the current proportion of girls which is just below 50%. So the random variable G = the number of girls in a family of 4 children where $G \sim B(4, 0.5)$ should provide a suitable model in this case.

(c) Let the random variable R represent the number of red balls picked. The number of trials is fixed as 3 balls are to be picked, so $n = 3$. Also, each trial is either a success (red) or a failure (white) but the method of selecting the balls is all important here. If the balls are selected *without replacement* then the probability of a red ball is not constant. If the balls are selected *with replacement* then the probability of selecting a red ball is $\frac{1}{4}$, the trials are independent and $R \sim B(3, \frac{1}{4})$.

Exercise 1C

1 The random variable $X \sim B(8, \frac{1}{3})$, find:
   (a) $P(X = 2)$ (b) $P(X \leqslant 2)$ (c) $P(X \geqslant 2)$

2 The random variable $Y \sim B(6, \frac{1}{4})$, find:
   (a) $P(Y = 3)$ (b) $P(Y < 3)$ (c) $P(Y > 3)$

3 The random variable $T \sim B(12, 0.6)$, find:
   (a) $P(T = 6)$ (b) $P(T = 9)$ (c) $P(6 \leqslant T \leqslant 9)$

4 The random variable $U \sim B(16, 0.2)$, find:
   (a) $P(U = 4)$ (b) $P(U < 4)$ (c) $P(U > 4)$.

5 The random variable $W \sim B(10, 0.35)$, find:
   (a) $P(W \leqslant 6)$ (b) $P(W \geqslant 5)$ (c) $P(W = 6)$
   (d) $P(4 \leqslant W \leqslant 7)$

6 A fair cubical die is rolled 5 times and the number of sixes is counted. Find the probability of:
   (a) no sixes   (b) at least one six   (c) no more than 4 sixes.

7 Four fair coins are tossed and the total number of heads showing is counted. Find the probability of:

(a) only one head   (b) at least one head

(c) the number of heads equalling the number of tails.

8 A balloon manufacturer claims that 95% of his balloons will not burst when blown up. If you have 20 of these balloons to blow up for a birthday party:

(a) what is the probability that none of them burst when blown up?

(b) Find the probability that exactly two balloons burst.

There are 17 children coming to the party but you decide to blow up all 20 balloons as some spares might be helpful.

(c) What is the probability that there are enough balloons?

9 A student suggests using a binomial distribution to model the following situations. State any assumptions that must be made and give possible values for the parameters n and p.

(a) A sample of 20 bolts is checked for defects from each large batch produced. The process should produce about 1% of defects.

(b) Some traffic lights have three phases: stop 48% of the time, wait or get ready 4% of the time and go 48% of the time. Assuming that you only cross a traffic light when it is in the go position, model the number of times that you have to wait or stop on your way to school given that there are 6 sets of traffic lights.

(c) When Stephanie plays tennis with Timothy on average one in every 8 of her serves is an 'ace'. How many 'aces' does Stephanie serve in the next 30 serves against Timothy?

10 State which of the following can be modelled with a binomial distribution and which can not. Reasons should be given.

(a) Given that 15% of people have blood that is Rhesus negative (Rh$^-$) model the number of pupils in a statistics class of 14 who are Rh$^-$.

(b) You are given a fair coin and told to keep tossing it until you obtain 4 heads in succession. Model the number of tosses you need.

(c) A certain car manufacturer produces 12% of new cars in the colour red, 8% blue, 15% white and the rest in other colours. You make a note of the colour of the first 15 new cars of this make. Model the number of red cars you observed.

11 A coin is biased so that a head is twice as likely to occur as is a tail. The coin is tossed repeatedly. Find the probability that:
(a) the first tail will occur on the fifth toss
(b) in the first seven tosses there will be exactly 2 tails. [E]

12 Team A has probability $\frac{2}{3}$ of winning whenever it plays. Given that A plays 4 games, find the probability that A wins more than half of the games. [E]

13 State the conditions under which the binomial distribution may be used. Illustrate your answer by referring to a specific example. Records kept in a hospital show that 3 out of every 10 casualties who come to the casualty department have to wait more than half an hour before receiving medical attention. Find, to 3 decimal places, the probability that of the first 8 casualties who come to that casualty department: (a) none, (b) more than two will have to wait more than half an hour before receiving medical attention. Find also the most probable number of the 8 casualties that will have to wait more than half an hour. [E]

14 A factory is considering two methods, I and II, of checking the quality of production of the batches of items it produces.
Method I consists of taking a random sample of 10 items from a large batch and accepting the batch if there are no defectives and rejecting the batch if there are two or more defectives. If there is one defective in the sample, another random sample of 10 items is taken from the batch. The batch is accepted if there are no defectives in this second sample and rejected otherwise.
Method II consists of taking a random sample of 20 items from a batch and accepting the batch if there is at most one defective in the sample. Otherwise the batch is rejected.
The factory knows that 1% of the items it produces are defective and wishes to use that method of checking the quality of production for which the probability of accepting a batch is the larger. Decide whether the factory should use Method I or Method II.
[E]

1.4 Mean and variance of a binomial distribution

Before we proceed to find the mean and variance of a binomial distribution, we are going to look back at exercise 8B, question 3 of Book S1. In this question you found the probability distribution for the sum of the scores on two fair dice. If X and Y represent the score on the first and second die respectively, then X and Y both have the same distribution with mean 3.5 and variance $\frac{35}{12}$. In the example referred to, you showed that the mean and variance for the sum $X + Y$ were 7 and $\frac{35}{6}$ respectively. This illustrates an important general result:

■ **If X and Y are two independent random variables then:**
$$\mathbf{E}(X + Y) = \mathbf{E}(X) + \mathbf{E}(Y)$$
$$\mathbf{Var}(X + Y) = \mathbf{Var}(X) + \mathbf{Var}(Y)$$

(Strictly speaking the independence is only required for the variance result.) A detailed knowledge of these formulae is not required for S2, but they can easily be extended to give the following formulae which will be very useful here.

■ $\mathbf{E}(X_1 + X_2 + \ldots + X_n) = \mathbf{E}(X_1) + \mathbf{E}(X_2) + \ldots + \mathbf{E}(X_n)$
  $\mathbf{Var}(X_1 + X_2 + \ldots + X_n) = \mathbf{Var}(X_1) + \mathbf{Var}(X_2) + \ldots + \mathbf{Var}(X_n)$

where the X_i are independent.

Consider the random variable $X \sim \mathrm{B}(n, p)$ and the random variables $Y_i (i = 1, 2, \ldots n)$ which represent the number of successes on the ith trial. The distribution of each of the Y_i will be the same:

y:	0	1
$\mathrm{P}(Y = y)$:	$1 - p$	p

It is easy to calculate:
$$\mathrm{E}(Y_i) = \sum y\, \mathrm{P}(Y = y) = 0 + (1 \times p) = p$$
and
$$\mathrm{Var}(Y_i) = \sum y^2\, \mathrm{P}(Y = y) - [\mathrm{E}(Y)]^2 = (1^2 \times p) - p^2 = p(1 - p)$$

Now X is the total number of successes in the n trials and so:
$$X = Y_1 + Y_2 + \ldots + Y_n$$

You can apply the above result to obtain:
$$\begin{aligned}
\mathrm{E}(X) &= \mathrm{E}(Y_1) + \mathrm{E}(Y_2) + \ldots + \mathrm{E}(Y_n) \\
&= p + p + \ldots + p \\
&= np
\end{aligned}$$
$$\begin{aligned}
\mathrm{Var}(X) &= \mathrm{Var}(Y_1) + \mathrm{Var}(Y_2) + \ldots + \mathrm{Var}(Y_n) \qquad (Y_i \text{ independent}) \\
&= p(1 - p) + p(1 - p) + \ldots + p(1 - p) \\
&= np(1 - p)
\end{aligned}$$

■ **If $X \sim B(n, p)$ then:**

$$E(X) = \mu = np$$
$$Var(X) = \sigma^2 = np(1-p) = npq$$

These results will be particularly useful in later work.

Example 6

A fair cubical die is thrown 36 times and the random variable X represents the number of sixes obtained.

(a) Find the mean and variance of X.
(b) Find $P(X < \mu - \sigma)$.

(a) The random variable $X \sim B(36, \frac{1}{6})$

$$\mu = E(X)$$
$$= 36 \times \frac{1}{6}$$
$$= 6$$
$$\sigma^2 = Var(X)$$
$$= 36 \times \frac{1}{6} \times \frac{5}{6}$$
$$= 5$$

(b) $P(X < \mu - \sigma) = P(X < 6 - \sqrt{5})$
$$= P(X < 3.763\ldots)$$
$$= P(X \leqslant 3)$$
$$= \left(\frac{5}{6}\right)^{36} + 36\left(\frac{5}{6}\right)^{35}\frac{1}{6} + 630\left(\frac{5}{6}\right)^{34}\left(\frac{1}{6}\right)^2 + 7140\left(\frac{5}{6}\right)^{33}\left(\frac{1}{6}\right)^3$$
$$= 0.0014\ldots + 0.0101\ldots + 0.0355\ldots + 0.0805\ldots$$
$$= 0.128 \text{ (3 d.p.)}$$

Exercise 1D

1 (a) Find the mean and variance of the random variable
$X \sim B(12, 0.25)$.
(b) Find $P(\mu - \sigma < X < \mu + \sigma)$.

2 (a) Find the mean and variance of the random variable
$Y \sim B(9, \frac{1}{3})$.
(b) Find $P(\mu - \sigma < Y \leqslant \mu)$.

3 It is estimated that 1 in 20 people are left-handed.
(a) What size sample should be taken to ensure that the expected number of left-handed people in the sample is 3?
(b) What is the standard deviation of the number of left-handed people in this case?

4 An experiment is conducted with a fair die to examine the number of sixes that occur. It is required to have the standard deviation smaller than 1. What is the largest number of throws that can be made?

5 The random variable X is distributed $B(n, p)$. For a fixed value of n find the value of p which maximises the variance of X.

6 State clearly conditions under which it is appropriate to assume that a random variable has a binomial distribution.

A door-to-door canvasser tries to persuade people to have a certain type of double-glazing installed. The probability that his canvassing at a house is successful is 0.05. Use tables of cumulative binomial probabilities, or otherwise, to find, to 4 decimal places, the probability that he will have at least 2 successes out of the first 10 houses he canvasses.

Find the number of houses he should canvass per day in order to average 3 successes per day.

Calculate the least number of houses that he must canvass in order that the probability of his getting at least one success exceeds 0.99.   [E]

1.5 The Poisson distribution

The exponential function e^x can be defined in a number of different ways and one, which is particularly helpful in statistics, is as a series expansion:

$$e^x = 1 + \frac{x}{1!} + \frac{x^2}{2!} + \frac{x^3}{3!} + \ldots + \frac{x^r}{r!} + \ldots$$

The series is infinite but most calculators have the facility to evaluate the exponential function to a reasonable degree of accuracy. So, for example, a calculator might give:

$$e^{0.5} = 1.648721271 \quad \text{and} \quad e^{-2} = 0.1353352832$$

See what your calculator shows for various value of x.

The definition above of e^x can be used to generate a probability distribution with parameter λ. Consider the series expansion for e^λ and remember that $\lambda^0 = 1$:

$$e^\lambda = \lambda^0 + \frac{\lambda^1}{1!} + \frac{\lambda^2}{2!} + \frac{\lambda^3}{3!} + \ldots + \frac{\lambda^r}{r!} + \ldots$$

Dividing both sides by e^{λ} gives:

$$1 = e^{-\lambda}\lambda^0 + \frac{e^{-\lambda}\lambda^1}{1!} + \frac{e^{-\lambda}\lambda^2}{2!} + \frac{e^{-\lambda}\lambda^3}{3!} + \ldots + \frac{e^{-\lambda}\lambda^r}{r!} + \ldots$$

Notice that the sum of the terms on the right-hand side equals 1 so you could use these values as probabilities to define a probability distribution. Let X be a random variable, such that X will take values in the set $\{0, 1, 2, 3, \ldots\}$. Thus the probability distribution of X is:

x:	0	1	2	3	$\ldots$	r	$\ldots$
$p(X = x)$:	$e^{-\lambda}$	$\dfrac{e^{-\lambda}\lambda}{1!}$	$\dfrac{e^{-\lambda}\lambda^2}{2!}$	$\dfrac{e^{-\lambda}\lambda^3}{3!}$	$\ldots$	$\dfrac{e^{-\lambda}\lambda^r}{r!}$	$\ldots$

and the probability function is:

$$P(X = r) = \frac{e^{-\lambda}\lambda^r}{r!} \qquad \text{where } r = 0, 1, 2, \ldots$$

Notice, once again, that this gives a *family* of distributions depending upon the value of the parameter λ. (The *binomial* distributions were dependent upon the two parameters n and p).

You now have a probability distribution but is it useful as a model in any particular situations and if so under what conditions? This is a particularly useful distribution known as the **Poisson distribution** and is named after the French mathematician Siméon Poisson. As with the binomial distribution there are certain conditions which must be satisfied if a Poisson distribution is to provide a suitable model in a particular situation. The Poisson distribution, as described above, can be *derived* from these conditions but that requires a level of mathematics beyond the scope of this course; however it is important that you have a feel for these conditions so that you can decide when a Poisson distribution might be an appropriate model.

Conditions for a Poisson distribution:
If X is the number of occurrences of a particular event in an interval of fixed length in space or time, then the events occur:

- **independently** of each other
- **singly** in continuous space or time
- at a **constant rate** in the sense that the mean number in an interval is proportional to the length of the interval.
  [Such events are sometimes called *random* or *rare* events.]

For example, a Poisson distribution should provide a good model for the number of radioactive particles being emitted by a certain source during a 5 minute period or the number of red cars passing your school or college gates in a 10 minute period. In both of these cases it is reasonable to assume that the events (radioactive particles or red cars) occur independently and singly (ignore the possibility of a car carrier with several red cars on board!) and at a constant rate in the sense that it is reasonable to assume that the events occur at a certain rate per minute.

Before you can use a Poisson distribution as a model though you need to know more about the parameter λ. It can be shown, but again the level of mathematics is a little beyond this course, that if the random variable X has a Poisson distribution with parameter λ then the mean and variance of X are both equal to λ.

1.6 The mean and variance of the Poisson distribution

■ **If X has a Poisson distribution with parameter λ then:**
$$\mu = E(X) = \lambda$$
$$\sigma^2 = Var(X) = \lambda$$

This important property of λ completes the definition of the Poisson distribution as a model to describe the occurrences of particular events that satisfy the above conditions.

■ **If X is the number of events that occur at random in a certain interval and λ is the *average* or *mean* number of events that occur in the interval then X has a Poisson distribution with parameter λ and probability function:**

$$P(X=r) = \frac{e^{-\lambda}\lambda^r}{r!} \qquad r = 0, 1, 2, 3, \ldots$$

X has a Poisson distribution with parameter λ is written as:

$$X \sim Po(\lambda)$$

Example 7
The number of telephone calls received at an exchange during a weekday morning follows a Poisson distribution with a mean of 6 calls per five minute period. Find the probability that:

(a) there are no calls in the next five minutes
(b) 3 calls are received in the next five minutes
(c) fewer than 2 calls are received between 11:00 and 11:05
(d) more than 2 calls are received between 11:30 and 11:35.

$\lambda = 6$ (= the mean number of calls in a five minute interval).

X = the number of calls received in a five minute period.

$$\therefore \qquad\qquad X \sim \text{Po}(6)$$

(a) $P(X = 0) = e^{-6} = 0.0025$ (4 d.p.)

(b) $P(X = 3) = \dfrac{e^{-6} \times 6^3}{3!} = 0.0892$ (4 d.p.)

(c) $P(X < 2) = P(X = 0) + P(X = 1)$

$$= e^{-6} + e^{-6} \times 6$$

$$= e^{-6}(1 + 6)$$

$$= 0.0174 \ (4 \text{ d.p.})$$

(d) $P(X > 2) = 1 - P(X \leqslant 2)$

$$= 1 - [P(X = 0) + P(X = 1) + P(X = 2)]$$

$$= 1 - e^{-6}(1 + 6 + 18)$$

$$= 1 - 25 \times e^{-6}$$

$$= 0.9380 \ (4 \text{ d.p.})$$

As with the binomial distribution there are tables of cumulative Poisson probabilities and these are particularly useful for calculations like those in part (d) of the above example. The Edexcel tables give $P(X \leqslant r)$ for values of r and particular values of λ, the mean of the distribution. So to complete part (d) of example 7, use $\lambda = 6$ and look up $P(X \leqslant 2)$ in the tables. This gives 0.0620 and subtracting this from 1 gives 0.9380, which matches the above working.

The tables are particularly useful if you need to work backwards. For example, if $X \sim \text{Po}(6.5)$ then to find the value of r so that $P(X \leqslant r) \geqslant 0.95$ is fairly straightforward from tables. From the tables:

$$P(X \leqslant 10) = 0.9332 \qquad \text{and} \qquad P(X \leqslant 11) = 0.9661$$

so that the value of r is 11. (Remember that the Poisson distribution is a *discrete* distribution taking whole numbers so the value of r must be an integer.)

Sometimes you may be given a rate of occurrence (for example, telephone calls arrive at a rate of 1.2 per minute) and have to calculate the value of λ appropriate to the interval you are using. Thus, for the above rate of 1.2 calls per minute you could calculate probabilities for the next four minute period by using $\lambda = 4 \times 1.2 = 4.8$.

Example 8

Some river water contains on average 500 bacteria per litre. A large bucket of the water is collected and after it has been well stirred a $1\,cm^3$ sample is examined.

(a) Find the probability of there being no bacteria in this sample.
(b) Find the probability of there being at least 4 bacteria in the sample.

Let λ be the average number of bacteria in $1\,cm^3$ of the water then:

$$\lambda = \tfrac{500}{1000} = 0.5$$

Let X be the number of bacteria in $1\,cm^3$ of the water.

Given that the water was well stirred before the sample was taken the bacteria should occur singly and independently so the Poisson distribution should provide a good model where $X \sim Po(0.5)$.

(a) $P(X = 0) = e^{-0.5} = 0.6065$ (4 d.p.)

(b) $P(X \geqslant 4) = 1 - P(X \leqslant 3)$
$= 1 - 0.9982$ (from tables)
$= 0.0018$ (4 d.p.)

Exercise 1E

1 If $X \sim Po(2.5)$, find:
   (a) $P(X = 1)$ (b) $P(X > 2)$ (c) $P(X \leqslant 5)$
   (d) $P(3 \leqslant X \leqslant 5)$

2 The random variable Y has a Poisson distribution with mean 4.5, find:
   (a) $P(Y = 2)$ (b) $P(Y \leqslant 1)$ (c) $P(Y > 4)$
   (d) $P(2 \leqslant Y \leqslant 6)$

3 The random variable $Y \sim Po(1.6)$, find:
   (a) $P(Y = 0)$ (b) $P(Y > 1)$ (c) $P(Y \leqslant 2)$
   (d) $P(1 < Y \leqslant 3)$

4 The random variable $Y \sim Po(0.8)$, find:
   (a) $P(Y \leqslant 1)$ (b) $P(Y > 2)$ (c) $P(1 < Y < 3)$
   (d) $P(2 < Y \leqslant 4)$

5 The random variable $X \sim Po(8.0)$, find the values of a, b, c and d so that:
   (a) $P(X \leqslant a) = 0.3134$ (b) $P(X \leqslant b) = 0.7166$
   (c) $P(X < c) = 0.0996$ (d) $P(X > d) = 0.8088$

6 The random variable $X \sim \text{Po}(3.5)$, find the values of a, b, c and d so that:

(a) $P(X \leqslant a) = 0.8576$ (b) $P(X > b) = 0.6792$

(c) $P(X \leqslant c) \geqslant 0.95$ (d) $P(X > d) \leqslant 0.005$

7 The random variable $X \sim \text{Po}(5.5)$, find the values of a, b, c and d so that:

(a) $P(X \leqslant a) \geqslant 0.90$ (b) $P(X \leqslant b) \geqslant 0.95$

(c) $P(X > c) \geqslant 0.90$ (d) $P(X > d) \leqslant 0.005$

8 The number of accidents which occur on a particular stretch of road on a given day is modelled by a Poisson distribution with mean 1.25. Find the probability that on this road on a particular day:

(a) no accidents occur

(b) at least two accidents occur.

9 A technician is responsible for a large number of machines. Minor adjustments have to be made to the machines and these occur at random and at a constant average rate of 7 per hour. Find the probability that:

(a) in a particular hour the technician makes four or fewer adjustments

(b) during a half-hour break no adjustments will be required.

10 A textile firm produces rolls of cloth but slight defects sometimes occur. The average number of defects per square metre is 2.5. Use a Poisson distribution to calculate the probability that:

(a) a $1.5\,\text{m}^2$ portion of cloth bought to make a skirt contains no defects

(b) a $4\,\text{m}^2$ portion of the cloth contains fewer than 5 defects.

(c) State briefly what assumptions have to be made before the Poisson distribution can be accepted as a suitable model in this situation.

11 State which of the following could possibly be modelled by a Poisson distribution and which can not. Give reasons for your answers.

(a) The number of misprints on this page in the first draft of this book.

(b) The number of pigs in a particular square metre of their field 1 hour after their feed was placed in a central trough.

(c) The number of pigs in a particular square metre of their field 1 minute after their feed was placed in a central trough.

(d) The amount of salt, in mg, contained in $1\,cm^3$ of water taken from a bucket immediately after a teaspoon of salt was added.

(e) The number of marathon runners passing the finishing post between 20 and 21 minutes after the winner of the race.

12 The number of accidents per week at a certain road intersection has a Poisson distribution with parameter 2.5. Find the probability that

(a) exactly 5 accidents will occur in a week

(b) more than 14 accidents will occur in 4 weeks. [E]

13 A shop sells a particular make of radio at a rate of 4 per week on average. The number sold in a week has a Poisson distribution.

(a) Find the probability that the shop sells at least 2 in a week.

(b) Find the smallest number that can be in stock at the beginning of a week in order to have at least a 99% chance of being able to meet all demands during that week. [E]

14 The number of accidents per week at a factory is a Poisson random variable with parameter 2.

(a) Find the probability that in any week chosen at random exactly 1 accident occurs.

(b) The factory is observed for 100 weeks. Determine the expected number of weeks in which 5 or more accidents occur. [E]

15 State the conditions under which a Poisson distribution is a suitable model to use in statistical work.

In a particular district it has been found, over a long period, that the number, X, of cases of measles reported per month has a Poisson distribution with parameter 1.5. Find, to 3 decimal places, the probability that in this district:

(a) in any given month, exactly 2 cases of measles will be reported

(b) in a period of 6 months, fewer than 10 cases of measles will be reported. [E]

16 During working hours an office switchboard receives telephone calls at random at an average rate of one call every 40 seconds.

(a) Find, to 3 decimal places, the probability that during a given one-minute period:

(i) no call is received

(ii) at least two calls are received

(b) Find, to 3 decimal places, the probability that no call is received between 10.30 a.m. and 10.31 a.m. and that at least two calls are received between 10.31 a.m. and 10.32 a.m.   [E]

17 State conditions under which the Poisson distribution is a suitable model to use in statistical work.

The number of typing errors per 1000 words made by a typist has a Poisson distribution with mean 2.5.

(a) Find, to 3 decimal places, the probability that in an essay of 4000 words there will be at least 12 typing errors.

The typist types 3 essays, each of length 4000 words.

(b) Find the probability that each contains at least 12 typing errors.   [E]

18 During office hours, telephone calls to a single telephone in an office come in at an average rate of 20 calls per hour. Assuming that a Poisson distribution is relevant, write down the probability function of X, the number of telephone calls arriving in each 5 minute period.

Find, to 3 decimal places, the probability that there will be

(a) fewer than 2 calls

(b) more than 3 calls in a 5 minute period.   [E]

1.7 The Poisson as an approximation to the binomial

A garden centre claims that only 5% of its daffodil bulbs will not produce flowers next season. You buy 100 of these bulbs and the random variable X represents the number of bulbs that do not flower, a suitable model for X is B(100, 0.05). Evaluating these probabilities can be rather awkward without the aid of a calculator and sometimes it is helpful to use the fact that the Poisson distribution provides an approximation to the binomial. In this example the average number of bulbs that do not flower is 5 (using np) and the events (a bulb not flowering) occur singly, independently and at a rate of 5 per season, so the conditions for a Poisson distribution are satisfied apart from the obvious fact that the sample space is different. A Poisson random variable takes values over the set $\{0, 1, 2, \ldots\}$ whereas our random variable X is defined over the set $\{0, 1, 2, \ldots, 100\}$. Because the value of n is large and the probabilities for large values of X are very small the Poisson distribution with mean 5 should provide a reasonable approximation to B(100, 0.05). The table below shows that there is a reasonable match particularly to 2 d.p.

$P(X = r)$	$X \sim B(100, 0.05)$	$X \sim Po(5)$
$r = 0$	0.0059	0.0067
$r = 1$	0.0312	0.0337
$r = 2$	0.0812	0.0842
$r = 3$	0.1395	0.1404
$r = 4$	0.1781	0.1755
$r = 5$	0.1800	0.1755
$r = 6$	0.1500	0.1462

This use of the Poisson distribution as an approximation to a binomial distribution improves the larger the value of n is and the smaller the value of p.

So, in summary:

- **Poisson as an *approximation* to the binomial**
  If $X \sim B(n, p)$ and
  – n is large
  – p is small
  then X can be approximated by Po(np).

Example 9

The probability that a wrapped chocolate biscuit is double wrapped is 0.01. Use a suitable approximation to find the probability that of the next 60 biscuits that you unwrap:

(a) none are double wrapped
(b) at least 2 are double wrapped.

Let X represent the number of biscuits that are double wrapped, then $X \sim B(60, 0.01)$. But n is quite large and p is small so $X \approx \sim Po(0.6)$. $[np = 60 \times 0.01 = 0.6]$

(a) $P(X = 0) \approx e^{-0.6} = 0.549$ (3 d.p.)

(b) $P(X \geqslant 2) = 1 - P(X \leqslant 1)$
$\approx 1 - e^{-0.6}[1 + 0.6]$
$= 1 - 0.8780\ldots$
$= 0.122$ (3 d.p.)

Notice that the answers using a binomial distribution in this case are (a) 0.547 and (b) 0.121.

Exercise 1F

1 In a certain manufacturing process the proportion of defective articles being produced is 2%. In a batch of 300 articles, find the probability that:
   (a) there are fewer than 2 defectives
   (b) there are exactly 4 defectives.

2 A medical practice screens a random sample of 250 of its patients for a certain condition which is present in 1.5% of the population. Find the probability that they obtained:
   (a) no patients with the condition
   (b) at least two patients with the condition.

3 An experiment involving two fair dice is carried out 180 times. The dice are placed in a container, shaken and the number of times a double six is obtained is recorded. Find the probability that the number of times a double six is obtained is:
   (a) once   (b) twice   (c) at least three.

4 It is claimed that 95% of the population in a certain village are right-handed. A random sample of 80 villagers are tested to see if they are right or left-handed. Use a Poisson approximation to estimate the probability that the number who are right-handed is:
   (a) 80   (b) 79   (c) at least 78.

5 In a computer simulation 500 dots were fired at a target and the probability of a dot hitting the target was 0.98. Find the probability that
   (a) all the dots hit the target   (b) at least 495 hit the target.

6 State the conditions under which the Poisson distribution may be used as an approximation to the binomial distribution.
   Independently for each call into the telephone exchange of a large organisation, there is a probability of 0.002 that the call will be connected to a wrong extension. Find, to 3 significant figures, the probability that, on a given day, exactly one of the first 5 incoming calls will be wrongly connected.
   Use a Poisson approximation to find, to 3 decimal places, the probability that, on a day when there are 1000 incoming calls, at least 3 of them are wrongly connected during that day.   [E]

7 State the conditions under which the binomial distribution $B(n, p)$ may be approximated by a Poisson distribution and write down the mean of this Poisson distribution.

Samples of blood were taken from 250 children in a region in India. Of these children, 4 had blood type *A2B*. Write down an estimate of p, the proportion of all children in this region having blood type *A2B*.

Consider a group of n children from this region and let X be the number with blood type *A2B*. Assuming that X is distributed $B(n, p)$ and that p has the value estimated above, calculate, to 3 decimal places, the probability that the number of children of blood type *A2B* in a group of 6 children from the region will be (a) zero, (b) more than one.

Use a Poisson approximation to calculate, to 4 decimal places, the probability that, in a group of 800 children from this region, there will be fewer than 3 children of blood type *A2B*.   [E]

8 State the conditions under which a Poisson distribution may be used as an approximation to the binomial distribution $B(n, p)$. Write down, in terms of n and p, the mean and the variance of the Poisson approximation.

Over a long period, a company finds that 2% of the gramophone records which it produces are faulty. A random sample of 15 records is taken from the production. Calculate, to 3 decimal places, the probability that there will be fewer than 2 faulty records in the sample.

Write down the mean number of faulty records in random samples of 15 taken from the production.

Using a Poisson approximation, or otherwise, find, to 3 decimal places, the probability that there will be at most 3 faulty records in a random sample of 100 records.   [E]

1.8 Selecting the appropriate distribution

A difficulty that you may experience is in deciding whether a Poisson or a binomial distribution is appropriate in a particular situation. There are some key features which you should look for which may help. In order to use a binomial distribution there must be a *finite* value for n, the number of trials and therefore the maximum value for the random variable, and a value for p, the constant probability of success. A Poisson distribution, by contrast, has no (theoretical) limit to the maximum value of the random variable but there must be a value for λ the *average* number of successes.

Some situations involve a mixture of binomial and Poisson distributions with one distribution providing a parameter for the next as the following example illustrates.

Example 10

A piece of machinery breaks down at an average rate of once a fortnight but these breakdowns occur randomly throughout a week.

(a) Find the probability of a week with no breakdowns.

A week with no breakdowns is called a star week. Every 12 weeks the number of star weeks is recorded and a report is sent to the machine manufacturers.

(b) Find the probability that there are more than 10 star weeks in the next report.

(a) The *average* rate is 0.5 per week, so a Poisson distribution is required. Let X represent the number of breakdowns per week then $X \sim \text{Po}(0.5)$

$$P(X = 0) = e^{-0.5}$$
$$= 0.6065\ldots$$
$$= 0.607 \text{ (3 d.p.)}$$

(b) Let Y represent the number of starred weeks in a period of 12 weeks. A value for n is 12 weeks and a value for p is your answer from part (a), so:

$$Y \sim \text{B}(12, 0.607)$$

$$P(Y > 10) = 12(0.607)^{11}(0.303) + (0.607)^{12}$$
$$= 0.01748\ldots$$
$$= 0.02 \text{ (2 d.p.)}$$

Notice that if you had used a more accurate value for the probability in (a) in the binomial calculation of (b) you would have obtained the value 0.0217 ... but to 2 d.p. the answers agree.

There are some questions of this type in Review exercise 1 and in the following exercise.

Exercise 1G

1 (a) State conditions under which the Poisson distribution is a suitable model to use in statistical work.

Flaws in a certain brand of tape occur at random and at an average of 0.75 per 100 metres. Assuming a Poisson distribution for the average number of flaws in a 400 metre roll of tape,

(b) find the probability that there will be at least one flaw.

(c) Show that the probability that there will be at most 2 flaws is 0.423 (to 3 decimal places).

In a batch of 5 rolls, each of length 400 metres.

(d) find the probability that at least 2 rolls will contain fewer than 3 flaws.

2 An archer fires arrows at a target and for each arrow, independently of all others, the probability that it hits the bull's eye is $\frac{1}{8}$.

(a) Given that the archer fires 5 arrows, find the probability that fewer than 2 arrows hit the bull's-eye.

The archer fires 5 arrows, collects them from the target and fires all 5 again.

(b) Find the probability that on both occasions fewer than 2 hit the bull's-eye.

The archer now fires 60 arrows at the target. Using a suitable approximation find

(c) the probability that fewer than 10 hit the bull's-eye,

(d) the smallest value of m such that the probability that the archer hits the bull's-eye with at least m arrows is greater than 0.5.

3 In Joe's roadside café $\frac{2}{5}$ of the customers buy a cup of tea.

(a) Find the probability that at least 4 of the next 10 customers will buy a cup of tea.

Joe has calculated that on a typical morning customers arrive in the café at an average rate of 0.5 per minute.

(b) Find the probability that at least 10 customers arrive in the next 15 minutes.

(c) Find the probability that exactly 10 customers arrive in the next 20 minutes.

(d) Find the probability that in the next 20 minutes exactly 10 customers arrive and at least 4 of them buy a cup of tea.

4 The number, X, of breakdowns per week of the lifts in a large block of flats has a Poisson distribution with a mean 0.25. Find, to 3 decimal places, the probability that on a particular week:

(a) there will be at least one breakdown

(b) there will be at most two breakdowns.

(c) Show that, to 3 decimal places, the probability that during a 12 week period there will be no lift breakdowns is 0.050.

The residents in the flats have a maintenance contract with *Liftserve*. The contract is for 20 blocks of 12 weeks. For every block of 12 weeks with no breakdowns the residents pay *Liftserve* £500. If there is at least 1 breakdown in a 12 week block then *Liftserve* will mend the lift free of charge and the residents pay nothing for the block of 12 weeks.

(d) Find the probability that over the period of the contract the residents pay no more than £1000.

5 Accidents occur in a school playground at the rate of 3 per year.

(a) Suggest a suitable model for the number of accidents in the playground in the next month.

(b) Using this model calculate the probability of 1 or more accidents in the playground in the next month.

6 A bakery claims that a pack of 10 of their teacakes contains on average 75 currants.

(a) Suggest a distribution that could be used to model the number of currants in a randomly selected teacake. State any assumptions that must be made for the model to be valid.

(b) Specify the value of any parameters.

(c) Show that the probability that a randomly selected teacake contains more than 7 currants is 0.475.

(d) Calculate the probability that in a pack of 10 teacakes at least 2 teacakes contain more than 7 currants.

7 A completely unprepared student is given a true/false type of test which contains 10 questions. What is the probability that the student will, by selecting answers at random, get all the answers right?

It is decided that a pass will be awarded for 8 correct answers. What is the probability of the student passing the test?

SUMMARY OF KEY POINTS

1 Binomial distribution

$$X \sim B(n,p)$$

$$P(X = r) = \binom{n}{r} p^r (1-p)^{n-r} \qquad r = 0, 1, \ldots n$$

$$\mu = E(X) = np$$

$$\sigma^2 = \text{Var}(X) = np(1-p) = npq$$

2 Poisson distribution

$$X \sim \text{Po}(\lambda)$$

$$P(X = r) = \frac{e^{-\lambda} \lambda^r}{r!}$$

$$\mu = E(X) = \lambda$$

$$\sigma^2 = \text{Var}(X) = \lambda$$

3 Poisson approximation to binomial

$$X \sim B(n,p)$$

if n is large
and p is small
then $X \approx \sim \text{Po}(np)$

Continuous random variables

2

2.1 The concept of a continuous random variable and its probability density function

In Book S1 chapter 8 you considered a continuous random variable H which represented the number of hours some batteries would last. The manufacturer specified that the batteries would last between 5 and 8 hours but did not provide information about how the probability is distributed over this range of values. Since H can take any value in the interval [5,8] you need to use a *continuous* function to describe the distribution. This is called a **probability density function** (p.d.f.) and it is denoted by f(x). It is usual to define f(x) over the range $(-\infty, \infty)$ and so f(x) = 0 for values of $x < 5$ and $x > 8$.

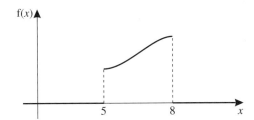

In another example in Book S1, the length of time to the nearest minute of each consultation with the doctor of 300 patients was as summarised below:

Time (to nearest minute)	Number of consultations	Relative frequency
2–3	30	0.10
4	96	0.32
5	48	0.16
6–7	84	0.28
8–10	27	0.09
11–15	15	0.05
Total	300	1.00

This gave the following relative frequency histogram:

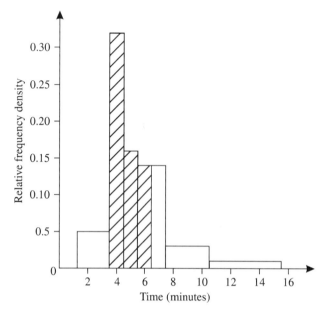

An important feature of a histogram like this is that the total area of the histogram is *equal to* 1. Furthermore the relative frequency is given by the area of the bar and not the height.

In Book S1 chapter 5, you used the idea of relative frequency as a way of defining probability and you could use this relative frequency histogram to find the probability that a consultation lasts between 4 and 6 minutes by calculating the shaded area of the histogram ($3\frac{1}{2}$ to $6\frac{1}{2}$, since the data is given to the nearest minute) which gives:

$$0.32 + 0.16 + \tfrac{1}{2}(0.28) = 0.62$$

A probability density function, f(x), gives a 'smooth' version of a relative frequency histogram and so f(x) will have two important properties:

f(x) $\geqslant 0$ $\forall x$ (this is equivalent to the result that probability $\geqslant 0$)

$$\int_{-\infty}^{\infty} f(x)\,dx = 1 \quad \text{or the area under the curve is 1}$$
$$\text{(compare } \sum p(x) = 1).$$

The probability density function of a continuous random variable is providing a *model* of a relative frequency histogram and so to *calculate probabilities for a continuous random variable you need to find an area* under the probability density function.

■ **If X is a continuous random variable with p.d.f. f(x)**

$$\mathbf{f(x) \geqslant 0 \ \ \forall x}$$

$$\int_{-\infty}^{\infty} \mathbf{f(x)\,dx = 1}$$

$$\mathbf{P(a < X < b) = \int_{a}^{b} f(x)\,dx}$$

The probability that a continuous random variable X lies between x and $x + \delta x$ will give an approximation to p(x) for a discrete distribution and from the diagram below you can see that this is approximately f(x) δx.

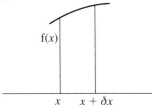

This leads to a useful parallel between results for discrete and continuous random variables. In the case of a discrete random variable:

$$\sum \text{p}(x) = 1$$

whereas for a continuous random variable:

$$\int \text{f}(x)\,\text{d}x = 1$$

So you can replace

$$\text{p}(x) \text{ by } \text{f}(x)\,\text{d}x \quad \text{and} \quad \sum \text{ by } \int.$$

Example 1

Identify which of the following could represent a probability density function. If it could not be a probability density function state why, and if it could then give the value of k and sketch it for all values of x.

(a) $\text{f}(x) = \begin{cases} kx(x - 2), & 1 \leqslant x \leqslant 3, \\ 0, & \text{otherwise.} \end{cases}$

(b) $\text{f}(x) = \begin{cases} kx(4 - x), & 2 \leqslant x \leqslant 4, \\ 0, & \text{otherwise.} \end{cases}$

(a) Notice that: $\text{f}(1.5) = k1.5(-0.5) = -0.75k$
But $\qquad\qquad\quad \text{f}(2.5) = k2.5(0.5) = 1.25k$

So whatever the value of k, for some value of x in the range we have $\text{f}(x) < 0$.
Therefore $\text{f}(x)$ cannot be a probability density function.

(b) A rough sketch of $y = x(4 - x)$ is:

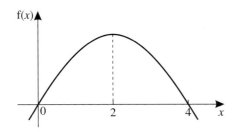

So for $k > 0$ we have $\text{f}(x) \geqslant 0$ for all values of x.

To find k we need to use the property $\int_2^4 f(x)\,dx = 1$.

So:
$$\int_2^4 k(4x - x^2)\,dx = 1$$

$$k\left[2x^2 - \frac{x^3}{3}\right]_2^4 = 1$$

$$k\left[\left(32 - \tfrac{64}{3}\right) - \left(8 - \tfrac{8}{3}\right)\right] = 1$$

$$k\left(\tfrac{16}{3}\right) = 1$$

so:
$$k = \tfrac{3}{16}$$

A sketch of $f(x)$ looks like this:

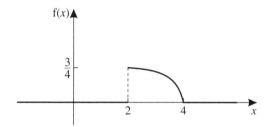

Notice that when you are asked to sketch a probability density function you should include the regions where $f(x) = 0$ either side of the main values of interest. A sketch should show the *shape* of the function and also have key values marked on each axis to illustrate the *scale*.

Exercise 2A

1 Decide whether a discrete or a continuous random variable can be used to describe the following.

(a) The height of a seedling in a biology experiment 14 days after planting.

(b) Your final mark in the S2 examination.

(c) The number of times the word "probability" occurs on a randomly selected page from this book.

(d) The time it would take you to run 100 m.

2 The following functions f(x) are proposed as probability density functions. In each case state whether or not they could provide a suitable probability density function.

(a)   (b)   (c)

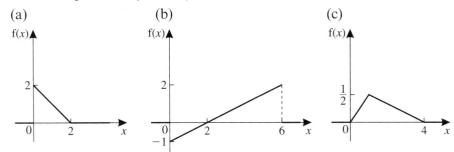

3 Find the value of k so that the following are valid probability functions.

(a) $f(x) = \begin{cases} kx, & 1 \leqslant x \leqslant 2, \\ 0, & \text{otherwise.} \end{cases}$

(b) $f(x) = \begin{cases} k(2-x), & 0 \leqslant x \leqslant 2, \\ 0, & \text{otherwise.} \end{cases}$

4 Find the value of a so that the following can represent a p.d.f.

(a) $g(x) = \begin{cases} ax^2, & 0 \leqslant x \leqslant 2, \\ 0, & \text{otherwise.} \end{cases}$

(b) $h(x) = \begin{cases} a(1+x^2), & -2 \leqslant x \leqslant 2, \\ 0, & \text{otherwise.} \end{cases}$

5 Find the value of a so that the following represent p.d.fs.

(a)   (b)   (c)

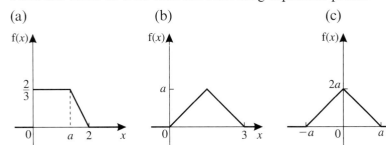

6 Describe which of the following could represent a p.d.f. and give a reason for your choice:

(a) $f(x) = \begin{cases} \frac{1}{5}x, & -1 \leqslant x \leqslant 3, \\ 0, & \text{otherwise.} \end{cases}$

(b) $f(x) = \begin{cases} x^2, & 0 \leqslant x \leqslant 2, \\ 0, & \text{otherwise.} \end{cases}$

(c) $f(x) = \begin{cases} \frac{3}{2}(x-1)^2, & 0 \leqslant x \leqslant 2, \\ 0, & \text{otherwise.} \end{cases}$

7 Explain why the following cannot represent probability density functions

(a) $f(x) = \begin{cases} k(3 - 2x), & 1 \leqslant x \leqslant 2, \\ 0, & \text{otherwise.} \end{cases}$

(b) $f(x) = \begin{cases} x^2, & -1 \leqslant x \leqslant 1, \\ 0, & \text{otherwise.} \end{cases}$

(c) $f(x) = \begin{cases} (x - 1)(2 - x), & 1 \leqslant x \leqslant 2, \\ 0, & \text{otherwise.} \end{cases}$

8 Some of the following could represent a p.d.f. and others could not. For those that could, find the value of k.

(a) $f(x) = \begin{cases} k(x + x^2), & -1 \leqslant x \leqslant 1, \\ 0, & \text{otherwise.} \end{cases}$

(b) $f(x) = \begin{cases} k(1 - x^2), & -1 \leqslant x \leqslant 1, \\ 0, & \text{otherwise.} \end{cases}$

(c) $f(x) = \begin{cases} k - x^3, & 0 \leqslant x \leqslant 2, \\ 0, & \text{otherwise.} \end{cases}$

9 Find equations for the following p.d.f.s, defining them for the range $-\infty < x < \infty$.

(a)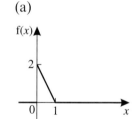

(b)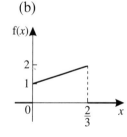

(c)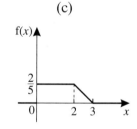

10 Sketch the following p.d.f.s.

(a) $f(x) = \begin{cases} \frac{2}{9}(4 - x), & 1 \leqslant x \leqslant 4, \\ 0, & \text{otherwise.} \end{cases}$

(b) $f(x) = \begin{cases} \frac{1}{4}x^3, & 0 \leqslant x \leqslant 2, \\ 0, & \text{otherwise.} \end{cases}$

(c) $f(x) = \begin{cases} \frac{1}{36}(9 - x^2), & -3 \leqslant x \leqslant 3, \\ 0, & \text{otherwise.} \end{cases}$

(d) $f(x) = \begin{cases} \frac{1}{9}x, & 0 \leqslant x \leqslant 3, \\ \frac{1}{9}(6 - x), & 3 \leqslant x \leqslant 6, \\ 0, & \text{otherwise.} \end{cases}$

2.2 The cumulative distribution function

In Book S1 cumulative frequency polygons were discussed and here the same idea is extended to probability distributions. The cumulative distribution function (c.d.f.) is defined as follows:

■ The **cumulative distribution function** $F(x_0)$ of the random variable X is:

$$F(x_0) = P(X \leqslant x_0)$$

You will recall from Book S1 that if X has a discrete distribution then $F(x_0)$ is simply given by:

$$F(x_0) = \sum_{x \leqslant x_0} p(x)$$

It is in connection with continuous random variables that the cumulative distribution function (c.d.f.) is most useful.

If X has a continuous distribution with probability density function (p.d.f.) $f(x)$, then the c.d.f. $F(x_0)$ is given by:

$$F(x_0) = \int_{-\infty}^{x_0} f(x)\, dx$$

Notice the link with the formula for the discrete random variables: $p(x)$ is replaced by $f(x)\, dx$ and $\sum$ by $\int$.

We use the notation $F(x)$ (i.e. capital 'F') for the c.d.f. but $f(x)$ (i.e. small 'f') for the p.d.f. There is an important connection between these two functions:

■ **If X is a continuous random variable with c.d.f. $F(x)$ and p.d.f. $f(x)$**

$$f(x) = \frac{d}{dx} F(x)$$

This result depends upon the relationship between integration and differentiation.

The c.d.f. is obtained by *integrating* the p.d.f.

so the p.d.f. can be obtained by *differentiating* the c.d.f.

Care should be taken when forming the c.d.f. that the correct limits are applied in the integration.

The random variable X has probability density function

$$f(x) = \begin{cases} \frac{1}{2}x, & 0 \leqslant x \leqslant 2, \\ 0, & \text{otherwise.} \end{cases}$$

You can find the cumulative distribution function as follows. From the definition:

$$F(x_0) = P(X \leqslant x_0)$$
$$= \int_{-\infty}^{x_0} f(x)\, dx$$

but over the interval $(-\infty, 0)$ $f(x)$ is zero, so $F(x_0)$ will also be zero for this interval. The interval of interest is $[0,2]$ and here $f(x)$ is given by $\frac{1}{2}x$, so the cumulative distribution function is given by:

$$F(x_0) = P(X \leqslant x_0)$$
$$= \int_{0}^{x_0} \tfrac{1}{2}x\, dx$$
$$= \left[\frac{1}{2}\frac{x^2}{2}\right]_0^{x_0} = \frac{x_0^2}{4}$$

You need to be able to define $F(x_0)$ over the whole range $(-\infty, \infty)$ and, since $F(x_0)$ will be equal to 1 for any value of x_0 greater than 2, you can write $F(x_0)$ as follows:

$$F(x_0) = \begin{cases} 0, & x_0 < 0, \\[2mm] \dfrac{x_0^2}{4}, & 0 \leqslant x_0 \leqslant 2, \\[2mm] 1, & x_0 > 2. \end{cases}$$

Example 2
The continuous random variable X takes values in the range $[0,2]$ and

$$P(X \leqslant x_0) = \frac{3x_0}{4} - \frac{x_0^3}{16} \qquad (0 \leqslant x_0 \leqslant 2)$$

(a) Find the probability density function $f(x)$.
(b) Sketch $f(x)$ and the cumulative distribution function.

(a) Differentiating $P(X \leqslant x_0) = F(x_0)$ gives:

$$\tfrac{3}{4} - \tfrac{3}{16}x_0^2$$

$$\therefore \qquad f(x) = \begin{cases} \tfrac{3}{4} - \tfrac{3}{16}x^2, & 0 \leqslant x \leqslant 2, \\[2mm] 0, & \text{otherwise.} \end{cases}$$

(b)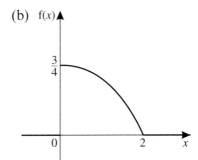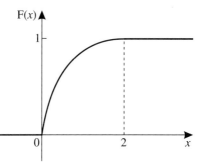

It is worth remembering that $F(x)$, the cumulative distribution function will always satisfy the following properties:

■ **If $F(x)$ is the c.d.f. of a continuous random variable X:**

$$0 \leqslant F(x) \leqslant 1$$

The gradient of $F(x)$ is never negative.

The c.d.f is particularly useful for finding medians and quartiles of continuous random variables as we shall see in section 2.4. The c.d.f. is also a powerful tool for finding the distributions of certain functions of random variables (see question 10 in exercise 2B) but a proper treatment of this is beyond the scope of this book.

Exercise 2B

1 The continuous random variable X has c.d.f. given by

$$F(x) = \begin{cases} 0, & x < 1, \\ \frac{1}{2}(x-1), & 1 \leqslant x \leqslant 3, \\ 1, & x > 3. \end{cases}$$

  (a) Find $P(X \leqslant 2.5)$.

  (b) Find $P(X > 1.5)$.

  (c) Find $P(1.5 \leqslant X \leqslant 2.5)$.

2 The continuous random variable X has c.d.f. given by

$$F(x) = \begin{cases} 0, & x < 1, \\ \frac{1}{3}(x^2 - 1), & 1 \leqslant x < 2, \\ 1, & x \geqslant 2. \end{cases}$$

  (a) Find $P(X \leqslant 1.5)$.

  (b) Find the probability density function $f(x)$ and define it fully.

3 The random variable X has a p.d.f. given by

$$f(x) = \begin{cases} \frac{3}{8}x^2, & 0 \leqslant x < 2, \\ 0, & \text{otherwise.} \end{cases}$$

  (a) Find the c.d.f. of X.

  (b) Find $P(X \leqslant 1)$.

4 Find the p.d.f. for the random variables with the following c.d.f.s:

  (a) $F(x) = \begin{cases} 0, & x < 2, \\ \frac{1}{5}(x^2 - 4), & 2 \leqslant x \leqslant 3, \\ 1, & x > 3. \end{cases}$

  (b) $F(x) = \begin{cases} 0, & x < 1, \\ \frac{1}{9}(2x^3 - 5x + 3), & 1 \leqslant x \leqslant 2, \\ 1, & x > 2. \end{cases}$

5 Find the values of a so that the following could be valid c.d.f.s.

(a) $F(x) = \begin{cases} 0, & x < 0, \\ \frac{1}{8}(x^2 + ax), & 0 \leqslant x \leqslant 2, \\ 1, & x > 2. \end{cases}$

(b) $F(x) = \begin{cases} 0, & x < a, \\ 1 + 2x, & a \leqslant x \leqslant 0, \\ 1, & x > 0. \end{cases}$

6 (a) Find the value of a and the value of b so that the following is a valid c.d.f.

$F(x) = \begin{cases} 0, & x < 1, \\ \frac{1}{b}(2x^3 + ax - 2a), & 1 \leqslant x \leqslant 3, \\ 1, & x > 3. \end{cases}$

(b) Find the p.d.f. and sketch it.

7 The continuous random variable X has a c.d.f. given by

$F(x) = \begin{cases} 0, & x < 1, \\ \frac{1}{2}(x^3 - 2x^2 + x), & 1 \leqslant x \leqslant 2, \\ 1, & x > 2. \end{cases}$

(a) Find the p.d.f. and sketch it.
(b) Find $P(X < 1.5)$.

8 Some of the following are possible c.d.f.s and some are not. If the function is a valid c.d.f. find the p.d.f., and if not explain why.

(a) $F(x) = \begin{cases} 0, & x < 0, \\ 3x - 2x^2, & 0 \leqslant x \leqslant 1, \\ 1, & x > 1. \end{cases}$

(b) $F(x) = \begin{cases} 0, & x < 0, \\ \frac{1}{2}(7x - 3x^2), & 0 \leqslant x \leqslant 2, \\ 1, & x > 2. \end{cases}$

(c) $F(x) = \begin{cases} 0, & x < 0, \\ \frac{1}{2}(5x^3 - 3x^5), & 0 \leqslant x \leqslant 1, \\ 1, & x > 1. \end{cases}$

(d) $F(x) = \begin{cases} 0, & x < 2, \\ \frac{1}{8}(6x - x^2), & 2 \leqslant x \leqslant 4, \\ 1, & x > 4. \end{cases}$

9 Find the c.d.f. for the random variable X with the following probability density function:

(a) $f(x) = \begin{cases} \frac{1}{36}(9 - x^2), & -3 \leqslant x \leqslant 3, \\ 0, & \text{otherwise.} \end{cases}$

(b) $f(x) = \begin{cases} \frac{1}{9}x, & 0 < x < 3, \\ \frac{1}{9}(6 - x), & 3 \leqslant x \leqslant 6, \\ 0, & \text{otherwise.} \end{cases}$

10 [This question is not typical of the type of question you might expect in S2 but it illustrates how the c.d.f. can be used in more advanced work.]

The random variable X has p.d.f. given by

$f(x) = \begin{cases} \frac{1}{2}x, & 0 \leqslant x \leqslant 2, \\ 0, & \text{otherwise.} \end{cases}$

(a) Find the c.d.f. of X, $F_X(x)$.

The random variable $Y = X^2$ and takes values over the range $0 \leqslant y \leqslant 4$.

(b) Show that $P(Y < y) = P(X \leqslant \sqrt{y})$.

(c) Hence show that the c.d.f. of Y, $F_Y(y)$ is given by

$F_Y(y) = \begin{cases} 0, & y < 0, \\ \frac{1}{4}y, & 0 \leqslant y \leqslant 4, \\ 1, & y > 4. \end{cases}$

(d) Hence find the p.d.f. of Y and sketch it.

2.3 The mean and variance of a continuous random variable

The mean μ for a *discrete* random variable X is given by:

$$\mu = E(X) = \sum_{\forall x} x p(x)$$

> **Remember:** $p(x)$ means $P(X = x)$

So for a *continuous* random variable X you can find the mean by replacing

$$\sum_{\forall x} \text{ by } \int_{-\infty}^{\infty} \quad \text{and} \quad p(x) \text{ by } f(x)\,dx$$

to obtain:

$$\mu = E(X) = \int_{-\infty}^{\infty} x f(x)\,dx$$

In the same way, the variance of the *discrete* random variable X is given by:

$$\sigma^2 = \text{Var}(X) = \sum_{\forall x} x^2 \text{p}(x) - \mu^2$$

So for a *continuous* random variable X you have:

$$\sigma^2 = \text{Var}(X) = \int_{-\infty}^{\infty} x^2 \text{f}(x) \, \text{d}x - \mu^2$$

■ **If X is a continuous random variable with p.d.f. f(x):**

$$\mu = \text{E}(X) = \int_{-\infty}^{\infty} x\text{f}(x) \, \text{d}x$$

$$\sigma^2 = \text{Var}(X) = \int_{-\infty}^{\infty} x^2 \text{f}(x) \, \text{d}x - \mu^2 = \text{E}(X^2) - [\text{E}(X)]^2$$

Example 3

A random variable X has probability density function

$$\text{f}(x) = \begin{cases} kx, & 0 \leqslant x \leqslant 1, \\ 0, & \text{otherwise.} \end{cases}$$

where k is a positive constant.

Find: (a) k (b) $\text{E}(X)$ (c) $\text{Var}(X)$.

A sketch of the p.d.f. looks like this:

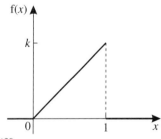

(a) To find k, use $\int_{-\infty}^{\infty} \text{f}(x) \, \text{d}x = 1$.

From the sketch this means finding the area of the triangle, so:

$$\tfrac{1}{2} \times 1 \times k = 1$$

$\Rightarrow \qquad\qquad \tfrac{1}{2}k = 1$

i.e. $\qquad\qquad k = 2$

(b) $$\text{E}(X) = \int_0^1 x2x \, \text{d}x$$

$$= \left[\frac{2x^3}{3} \right]_0^1$$

$$= \tfrac{2}{3} - 0$$

$$= \tfrac{2}{3}$$

(c)
$$E(X^2) = \int_0^1 x^2\, 2x\, dx$$
$$= \left[\frac{2x^4}{4}\right]_0^1$$
$$= \tfrac{1}{2} - 0$$
$$= \tfrac{1}{2}$$
$\therefore$
$$Var(X) = \tfrac{1}{2} - \left(\tfrac{2}{3}\right)^2$$
$$= \tfrac{1}{18}$$

Notice the form in which a p.d.f. is usually defined. In this example the main range of interest was the interval [0,1] but f(x) was defined for all real values of x. It is always worth drawing a sketch of the p.d.f. as this can often shorten the subsequent working. In this example k was easily found using the geometry of the p.d.f. rather than integration.

Example 4

The continuous random variable Y has probability density function

$$f(y) = \begin{cases} \frac{3}{32}[4 - y^2], & -2 \leqslant y \leqslant 2, \\ 0, & \text{otherwise.} \end{cases}$$

(a) Find $E(Y)$.
(b) Show that $Var(Y) = \frac{4}{5}$.
(c) Find $P(Y > 1)$.

The p.d.f. is part of a parabola and can be sketched as:

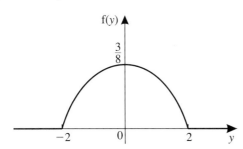

(a) By symmetry: $\qquad E(Y) = 0$

(b) $\qquad Var(Y) = E(Y^2) - 0^2 = \frac{3}{32}\int_{-2}^{2}(4y^2 - y^4)\, dy$

$$= \frac{3}{32}\left[\frac{4}{3}y^3 - \frac{1}{5}y^5\right]_{-2}^{2}$$

$$= \left(1 - \tfrac{3}{5}\right) - \left(-1 + \tfrac{3}{5}\right)$$

$$= \tfrac{4}{5}$$

(c)
$$P(Y > 1) = \tfrac{3}{32} \int_1^2 (4 - y^2) \, dy$$

$$= \tfrac{3}{32} \left[4y - \tfrac{1}{3}y^3 \right]_1^2$$

$$= \left(\tfrac{3}{4} - \tfrac{1}{4} \right) - \left(\tfrac{3}{8} - \tfrac{1}{32} \right)$$

$$= \tfrac{16 - 12 + 1}{32}$$

$$= \tfrac{5}{32}$$

Exercise 2C

1 A random variable X has p.d.f. $f(x)$ given by:
$$f(x) = \begin{cases} k(1 - x), & 0 \leqslant x \leqslant 1, \\ 0, & \text{otherwise.} \end{cases}$$
where k is a positive constant.

(a) Find k.

(b) Find $E(X)$.

(c) Show that $\text{Var}(X) = \tfrac{1}{18}$.

(d) Find $P(X > \mu)$.

2 The random variable Y has p.d.f. given by:
$$f(y) = \begin{cases} \tfrac{1}{3} + \tfrac{1}{6}y, & 0 \leqslant y \leqslant 2, \\ 0, & \text{otherwise.} \end{cases}$$

Find the following:

(a) $E(Y)$ (b) $\text{Var}(Y)$ (c) $P(Y < 1)$ (d) $P(Y > \mu)$.

3 The random variable X has p.d.f. given by:
$$f(x) = \begin{cases} 12x^2(1 - x), & 0 \leqslant x \leqslant 1, \\ 0, & \text{otherwise.} \end{cases}$$

(a) Find $P(X < \tfrac{1}{2})$.

(b) Find $E(X)$.

4 The random variable X has p.d.f. given by:
$$f(x) = \begin{cases} \tfrac{3}{8}(1 + x^2), & -1 \leqslant x \leqslant 1, \\ 0, & \text{otherwise.} \end{cases}$$

(a) Sketch the p.d.f. of X.

(b) Write down $E(X)$.

(c) Show that $\sigma^2 = 0.4$.

(d) Find $P(-\sigma < X < \sigma)$ to 2 d.p.

5 The random variable T has p.d.f. given by:

$$f(t) = \begin{cases} kt^3, & 0 \leqslant t \leqslant 2, \\ 0, & \text{otherwise.} \end{cases}$$

where k is a positive constant.
(a) Find k.
(b) Show that $E(T) = 1.6$.
(c) Find $P(T < 1)$.

6 Telephone calls arriving at a company are referred immediately by the receptionist to other people in the company. The duration of each call, in minutes, is modelled by a continuous random variable T, having probability density function

$$f(t) = \begin{cases} kt^2, & 0 \leqslant t \leqslant 10, \\ 0, & \text{otherwise.} \end{cases}$$

(a) Show that $k = 0.003$.
(b) Find the cumulative distribution function of T and specify it for all values of t.
(c) Find the probability of a call lasting between 7 and 9 minutes.
(d) Sketch the form of the probability density function.
A student observes the length of telephone calls to the switchboard and believes that the model is inappropriate.
(e) Sketch the shape of a probability density function that might be more realistic.

7 The random variable X has probability density function:

$$f(x) = \begin{cases} 3x^k, & 0 \leqslant x \leqslant 1, \\ 0, & \text{otherwise.} \end{cases}$$

where k is a positive integer.
Find:
(a) the value of k
(b) the mean of X. [E]

8 An agency rents out flats to holiday makers. The weekly rent, X tens of pounds, of the flats is a continuous random variable with probability density function given by:

$$f(x) = \begin{cases} kx(18 - x), & 6 \leqslant x \leqslant 15, \\ 0, & \text{otherwise.} \end{cases}$$

(a) Show that $k = \frac{1}{648}$.

(b) Calculate, to the nearest penny, the mean weekly rent.

(c) To book a flat with the agency, a holiday maker must pay a deposit of 10% of the weekly rent of the flat. Find, to the nearest penny, the mean deposit paid.

(d) In order to cover the agency's costs, the mean deposit needs to be £14. It is decided that on any flat with a weekly rent of more than £120 an *extra* fixed deposit of £D must be paid. Calculate the value of D correct to 2 decimal places. [E]

9 The queuing time, X minutes, of a traveller at the ticket office of a large railway station has probability density function, f, defined by:

$$f(x) = \begin{cases} kx(100 - x^2), & 0 \leqslant x \leqslant 10, \\ 0, & \text{otherwise.} \end{cases}$$

Find:

(a) the value of k

(b) the mean of the distribution

(c) the standard deviation of the distribution to 2 decimal places

(d) the probability that a traveller at the ticket office will have to queue for more than 2 minutes.

Given that 3 travellers go independently to the booking office, find, to 2 significant figures, the probability that one has to queue for less than one minute, one has to queue for between one and two minutes and one has to queue for more than two minutes. [E]

10 The continuous random variable Y has a probability density function:

$$f(y) = \begin{cases} \frac{1}{\pi}, & -\frac{\pi}{2} \leqslant y \leqslant \frac{\pi}{2}, \\ 0, & \text{otherwise.} \end{cases}$$

(a) Find the mean of Y.

(b) Find the variance of Y. [E]

2.4 Mode, median and quartiles of continuous random variables

The concepts of mode and median for a sample of data were discussed in Book S1 and the ideas introduced there are easily extended to continuous random variables. The probability density function shows how the probability is distributed and the **mode** is the value of the random variable X where it is most dense (note *mode* for *most* dense). A sketch of the p.d.f. is often helpful as sometimes the mode occurs at a stationary point but not always!

Consider the following random variables X and Y with probability distribution functions $f_1(x)$ and $f_2(y)$ respectively:

$$f_1 = \begin{cases} 12x^2(1-x), & 0 \leqslant x \leqslant 1, \\ 0, & \text{otherwise.} \end{cases} \qquad f_2 = \begin{cases} 2y, & 0 \leqslant y \leqslant 1, \\ 0, & \text{otherwise.} \end{cases}$$

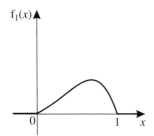
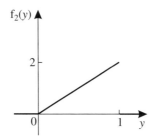

The mode of X gives rise to the maximum point on the p.d.f. $f_1(x)$. So by differentiation:

$$\frac{d}{dx}(12x^2 - 12x^3) = 0$$

$$\Rightarrow \qquad 12(2x - 3x^2) = 0$$

i.e. $$x(2 - 3x) = 0$$

$$\therefore \qquad x = \tfrac{2}{3}$$

From the sketch above this clearly gives the maximum so the mode of X is $\tfrac{2}{3}$. The mode of Y does not occur at a stationary point so differentiating the p.d.f. is no help but from the sketch you can see that the mode of Y is 1. Sometimes a random variable may not have a mode.

The cumulative distribution function (c.d.f.) is a useful tool for finding the **median** of a continuous random variable. The median value of the random variable X has 50% of the distribution below it and so a convenient way of finding the median, m, is to solve the equation $F(m) = \tfrac{1}{2}$.

■ **If X is a continuous random variable with c.d.f. $F(x)$, the median value m of X is given by:**

$$F(m) = \tfrac{1}{2}$$

You can also find the quartiles of a continuous random variable by solving the equation $F(q) = \frac{1}{4}$ to give the lower quartile, q_1, and $F(q) = \frac{3}{4}$ to find the upper quartile, q_3.

Example 5

The continuous random variable X has p.d.f. given by:

$$f(x) = \begin{cases} 4x - 4x^3, & 0 \leqslant x \leqslant 1, \\ 0, & \text{otherwise..} \end{cases}$$

(a) Find the mode of X.
(b) Find the c.d.f. of X.
(c) Find the $P(0.1 < X < 0.6)$.
(d) Find the median value of X.

A sketch of the p.d.f. is:

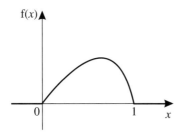

(a) The mode is clearly a stationary point, so set $\dfrac{\mathrm{d}}{\mathrm{d}x} f(x) = 0$

$\Rightarrow \qquad 4(1 - 3x^2) = 0$

$\Rightarrow \qquad\qquad x = \pm \frac{1}{\sqrt{3}}$ (but $-\frac{1}{\sqrt{3}}$ is outside the range)

; The mode of X is $\frac{1}{\sqrt{3}}$ or 0.577 (3 d.p.)

(b) The c.d.f. is given by:

$$F(x_0) = 4 \int_0^{x_0} (x - x^3) \,\mathrm{d}x$$

$$= \left[2x^2 - x^4 \right]_0^{x_0}$$

$$= 2x_0^2 - x_0^4$$

So $\qquad F(x) = \begin{cases} 0, & x < 0, \\ 2x^2 - x^4, & 0 \leqslant x \leqslant 1, \\ 1, & x > 1. \end{cases}$

(c) $P(0.1 < X < 0.6) = F(0.6) - F(0.1)$

$$= \{2 \times (0.6)^2 - (0.6)^4\} - \{2 \times (0.1)^2 - (0.1)^4\}$$

$$= 0.5705$$

(d) The median m is given by:

$$2m^2 - m^4 = 0.5$$

i.e. $$0 = 2m^4 - 4m^2 + 1$$

i.e. $$m^2 = \frac{4 \pm \sqrt{16 - 8}}{4}$$

$$= 1 \pm \frac{\sqrt{2}}{2}$$

But to be in the range the $-$ve is needed:

$$\therefore \qquad m = \sqrt{1 - \frac{\sqrt{2}}{2}}$$

$$= 0.541 (3 \text{ d.p.})$$

Exercise 2D

1 The random variable X has p.d.f. $f(x)$ given by:

$$f(x) = \begin{cases} 1 - \frac{1}{2}x, & 0 \leqslant x \leqslant 2, \\ 0, & \text{otherwise.} \end{cases}$$

(a) Sketch the p.d.f. of X.   (b) Write down the mode of X.

(c) Find the c.d.f. of X.   (d) Find the median value of X.

2 The random variable Y has p.d.f. $f(y)$ given by:

$$f(y) = \begin{cases} \frac{1}{2} - \frac{1}{9}y, & 0 \leqslant y \leqslant 3, \\ 0, & \text{otherwise.} \end{cases}$$

(a) Sketch the p.d.f. of Y.   (b) Write down the mode of Y.

(c) Find the c.d.f. of Y.   (d) Find the median value of Y.

3 The random variable X has p.d.f. given by:

$$f(x) = \begin{cases} \frac{1}{4}x^3, & 0 \leqslant x \leqslant 2, \\ 0, & \text{otherwise.} \end{cases}$$

(a) Sketch the p.d.f. of X.   (b) Write down the mode of X.

(c) Find the c.d.f. of X.   (d) Find the median value of X.

4 The random variable X has p.d.f. given by:

$$f(x) = \begin{cases} \frac{3}{8}(x^2 + 1), & -1 \leqslant x \leqslant 1, \\ 0, & \text{otherwise.} \end{cases}$$

(a) Sketch the p.d.f. of X.

(b) What can you say about the mode of X?

(c) Write down the median value of X.

(d) Find the c.d.f. of X.

5 The random variable X has p.d.f. given by:

$$f(x) = \begin{cases} \frac{3}{32}(4 - x^2), & -2 \leqslant x \leqslant 2, \\ 0, & \text{otherwise.} \end{cases}$$

(a) Sketch the p.d.f. of X.

(b) Write down the mode and median of X.

(c) Find the c.d.f. of X.

6 The random variable X has p.d.f. given by:

$$f(x) = \begin{cases} \frac{3}{10}(3x - x^2), & 0 \leqslant x \leqslant 2, \\ 0, & \text{otherwise.} \end{cases}$$

(a) Sketch the p.d.f. of X.

(b) Find the mode of X.

(c) Find the c.d.f. of X.

(d) Show that the median of X lies between 1.23 and 1.24.

7 The c.d.f. of a random variable X is given by:

$$F(x) = \begin{cases} 0, & x < 0, \\ 4x^3 - 3x^4, & 0 \leqslant x \leqslant 1, \\ 1, & x > 1. \end{cases}$$

(a) Find the p.d.f. of the random variable X.

(b) Find the mode of X.

(c) Find $P(0.2 < X < 0.5)$.

8 The c.d.f. of a random variable X is given by:

$$F(x) = \begin{cases} 0, & x < 1, \\ \frac{1}{8}(x^2 - 1), & 1 \leqslant x \leqslant 3, \\ 1, & x > 3. \end{cases}$$

(a) Find the p.d.f. of the random variable X.

(b) Find the mode of X.

(c) Find the median of X.

(d) Find the quartiles of X.

9 The mode of a continuous random variable X is 1 and this is a stationary point. Given that X takes values over the range $[0,3]$ find possible expressions for:

(a) the c.d.f. of X (b) the p.d.f. of X.

10 The amount of vegetables eaten by a family in a week is a random variable W kg. The probability density function is given by:

$$f(w) = \begin{cases} \frac{20}{5^5}w^3(5 - w), & 0 \leqslant w \leqslant 5, \\ 0, & \text{otherwise.} \end{cases}$$

Continuous random variables**57**

(a) Find the cumulative distribution function of W.

(b) Find, to 3 decimal places, the probability that the family eats between 2 kg and 4 kg of vegetables in one week.

(c) Verify that the amount, m, of vegetables such that the family is equally likely to eat more or less than m in any week is about 3.431 kg. [E]

11 A continuous random variable X has probability density function, f, defined by

$$f(x) = \begin{cases} \frac{1}{4}, & 0 \leqslant x < 1, \\ \dfrac{x^3}{5}, & 1 \leqslant x \leqslant 2, \\ 0, & \text{otherwise.} \end{cases}$$

Obtain the cumulative distribution function and hence, or otherwise, find, to 3 decimal places, the median and the interquartile range of the distribution. [E]

SUMMARY OF KEY POINTS

1 **Continuous random variable X**

$$\int_{-\infty}^{\infty} f(x)\,dx = 1$$

$$\mu = E(X) = \int_{-\infty}^{\infty} xf(x)\,dx$$

$$\sigma^2 = E(X^2) - \mu^2 = \int_{-\infty}^{\infty} x^2 f(x)\,dx - \mu^2$$

2 **Cumulative distribution function $F(x)$**

$$0 \leqslant F(X) \leqslant 1$$

$$F(x_0) = P(X \leqslant x_0) = \int_{-\infty}^{x_0} f(x)\,dx$$

Median m satisfies $F(m) = 0.5$

Quartile Q_1 satisfies $F(Q_1) = 0.25$

Quartile Q_3 satisfies $F(Q_3) = 0.75$

Review exercise 1

1 Which of the following are discrete random variables and which continuous?
   (a) Examination marks.
   (b) Heights of people.
   (c) Time waiting for a bus.
   (d) Turns on a fruit machine.
   (e) Prices of tins of paint.
   (f) Weight of a packet of cereal.
   (g) The diameters of ball bearings.

2 Which of the following variables is best modelled by a Poisson distribution and which is best modelled by a binomial distribution?
   (a) The number of hits by an arrow on a target.
   (b) The number of earth tremors that take place in a village over a given period of time.
   (c) The number of particles emitted per minute by a radioactive isotope.
   (d) The number of heads you get when tossing two coins several times.
   (e) The number of accidents in a city per year.
   (f) The number of flying bomb hits in specified areas in London in World War 2.

3 What is the relationship between the mean and variance of a Poisson distribution? List three conditions under which a Poisson distribution might be obtained.

4 *Computer Weekly* is found to have an average of 3 misprints per page. What is the probability that:
   (a) page 7 has no misprints
   (b) the last page has 6 misprints (the magazine has a total of 98 pages).

5 A probability density function is sketched below.

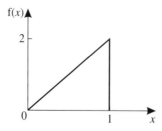

(a) Write down an expression for the probability density function $f(x)$.

(b) Find and draw a sketch of the cumulative distribution function.

(c) Work out the mean and median.

(d) What is $P(x \leqslant 0.5)$?

6 The random variable X has a binomial distribution B(10, 0.35). Find $P(X \leqslant 4)$.

The random variable Y has the Poisson distribution with mean 3.5. Find $P(2 < Y \leqslant 5)$. [E]

7 The random variable X has the probability density function given by:

$$f(x) = \begin{cases} kx, & 0 \leqslant x \leqslant 1, \\ k, & 1 < x \leqslant 2, \\ 0, & \text{otherwise.} \end{cases}$$

where k is a constant. Find:

(a) The value of k.

(b) $E(X)$ and $E(X^2)$.

(c) The median of X.

8 The borough of Esklington decided to do a study of accidents in the borough over a period of 1500 days. The results were as follows:

Accidents per day	0	1	2	3	4	5
Frequency	342	483	388	176	111	0

What theoretical distribution might be suitable as a model for these data?

Calculate using this model the expected frequencies for:

(a) no accident occurring in a given day

(b) less than three accidents occurring in a given day.

9 Loaves of bread on a production line pass a monitoring point at an average rate of 300 loaves per hour.
(a) How many loaves would you expect to pass the monitoring point in 2 minutes?
(b) What is the probability that none pass the monitoring point in any given minute?

10 (a) The probability that a component intended for use in a computer passes a purity test is 0.038. In a batch of 10 randomly selected components find, to 3 decimal places, the probability that:
(i) none of the components passes the test
(ii) fewer than three components pass the test.
(b) Using a suitable approximation, estimate the probability that fewer than four components in a batch of 100 pass the test. [E]

11 Two friends make regular telephone calls to each other. The duration, in minutes, of their telephone conversation is modelled by the random variable T, having probability density function

$$f(t) = \begin{cases} \frac{1}{150}(25 - t), & \text{for } 5 \leqslant t \leqslant 15, \\ 0, & \text{otherwise.} \end{cases}$$

(a) Sketch the probability density function of T.
(b) For all values of t, find the cumulative distribution function of T.
(c) Find the probability that a telephone conversation lasts longer than 12 minutes.
(d) Show that the median duration of a telephone conversation is given by $(25 - 5\sqrt{10})$ minutes.
(e) Give a reason why this initial model may not be realistic for the distribution of telephone conversations.
(f) Sketch the probability density function of a more realistic model. [E]

12 Seismic earth tremors occur at an active part of the earth's crust at the average rate of one every two days. What is the most likely number of tremors to occur in a week?

13 The probability distribution f(x) is sketched below

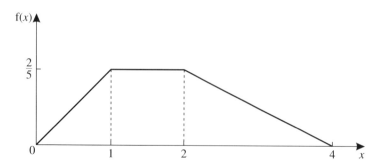

(a) Write down an expression for this distribution (X) and evaluate E(X).

(b) What is the probability that the variable lies between 2.5 and 3?

14 Accidents occur at a certain road junction at the average rate of 3 per year.

(a) Suggest a suitable model for the number of accidents at this junction in the next month.

(b) Show that, under this model, the probability of 2 or more accidents at this road junction in the next month is 0.0265 to 4 decimal places.

The local residents have applied for a crossing to be installed. The planning committee agree to monitor the situation for the next 12 months. If there is at least one month with 2 or more accidents in it they will install a crossing.

(c) Find the probability that a crossing is installed. [E]

15 A bag contains a large number of beads of which 45% are yellow. A random sample of 20 beads is taken from the bag. Use the binomial distribution to calculate the probability that the sample contains:

(a) fewer than 12 yellow beads

(b) exactly 12 yellow beads. [E]

16 The continuous random variable X has probability density function f(x) as follows:

$$f(x) = \begin{cases} k(4 - x), & 0 \leqslant x \leqslant 2, \\ 0, & \text{otherwise.} \end{cases}$$

(k is a constant)

(a) Find the value of k, E(X) and the standard deviation of X.

(b) Find the c.d.f. of X.

(c) Find the upper and lower quartiles and the median of X.

(d) Find $P(0.6 \leqslant X < 0.62)$.

17 (a) A discrete random variable X has the probability
function, $p(x)$, given by:

$$p(x) = \begin{cases} kx^2, & x = 0,\ 1,\ 2,\ 3, \\ 0, & \text{otherwise.} \end{cases}$$

Find the values of:

(i) k (ii) $E(X)$ (iii) $Var(X)$.

(b) A continuous random variable X has the probability
density function, $f(x)$, given by:

$$f(x) \begin{cases} kx^2, & 0 \leqslant x \leqslant 3, \\ 0, & \text{otherwise.} \end{cases}$$

Find the values of:

(i) k (ii) $E(X)$ (iii) $Var(X)$.

(iv) the median of X, to 3 significant figures.   [E]

18 Breakdowns occur on a particular machine at a rate of 2.5
per month. Assuming that the number of breakdowns can be
modelled by a Poisson distribution, find the probability that

(a) exactly 3 occur in a particular month

(b) more than 10 occur in a 3 month period

(c) exactly 3 occur in each of 2 successive months.   [E]

19 State, giving your reasons, the distribution which you would
expect to be appropriate in describing:

(a) the number of heads in 10 throws of a penny

(b) the number of blemishes per m^2 of sheet metal.

A building has an automatic telephone exchange. The number
X of wrong connections in one day is a Poisson variable with
parameter λ. Find, in terms of λ, the probability that in any
one day there will be:

(c) exactly 3 wrong connections

(d) 3 or more wrong connections.

Evaluate, to 3 decimal places, these probabilities when
$\lambda = 0.5$. Find, to 3 decimal places, the largest value of λ for
the probability of one or more wrong connections in any day
to be at most $\frac{1}{6}$.   [E]

20 A geography student is studying the distribution of
telephone boxes in a large rural area where there is an
average of 300 boxes per 500 km². A map of part of the
area is divided into 50 squares, each of area 1 km² and the
student wishes to model the number of telephone boxes per
square.

(a) Suggest a suitable simple model the student could use and
specify any parameters required,

One of the squares is picked at random.

(b) Find the probability that this square does not contain any
telephone boxes.

(c) Find the probability that this square contains at least 3
telephone boxes.

The student suggests using this model on another map of a
large city and surrounding villages.

(d) Comment, giving your reason briefly, on the suitability of
the model in this situation. [E]

21 The continuous random variable X has probability density
function:

$$f(x) = \begin{cases} \dfrac{1+x}{6}, & 1 \leqslant x \leqslant 3, \\ 0, & \text{otherwise.} \end{cases}$$

(a) Sketch the probability density function of X.
(b) Calculate the mean of X.
(c) Specify fully the cumulative distribution function of X.
(d) Find m such that $P(X \leqslant m) = \frac{1}{2}$. [E]

22 All the letters in a particular office are typed either by Pat, a
trainee typist, or by Lyn, who is a fully-trained typist. The
probability that a letter typed by Pat will contain one or more
errors is 0.3. Find the probability that a random sample of 4
letters typed by Pat will include exactly one letter free from error.
The probability that a letter typed by Lyn will contain one or
more errors is 0.05. Use tables, or otherwise, to find, to
3 decimal places, the probability that in a random sample of
20 letters typed by Lyn, not more than 2 letters will contain
one or more errors.

On any one day, 6% of the letters typed in the office are typed by Pat. One letter is chosen at random from those typed on that day. Show that the probability that it will contain one or more errors is 0.065.

Given that each of 2 letters chosen at random from the day's typing contains one or more errors, find, to 4 decimal places, the probability that one was typed by Pat and the other by Lyn. [E]

23 The lifetime in tens of hours, of a certain delicate electrical component is modelled by the random variable X with probability density function

$$f(x) = \begin{cases} k(9 - x), & 0 \leqslant x \leqslant 9, \\ 0, & \text{otherwise.} \end{cases}$$

where k is a positive constant.

(a) Show that $k = \frac{2}{81}$.

(b) Find the mean lifetime of a component.

(c) Show that the standard deviation of lifetimes is 21.2 hours.

(d) Find the probability that a component lasts at most 50 hours.

A particular device requires two of these components and it will not operate if one or more of the components fail. The device has just been fitted with two new components. The lifetime of components are independent.

(e) Find the probability that the device will work for more than 50 hours.

(f) Give a reason why the above distribution may not be realistic as a model for the distribution of lifetimes of these electrical components. [E]

24 The continuous random variable X has probability density function given by:

$$f(x) = \begin{cases} k(1 + x^2), & \text{for } 0 \leqslant x \leqslant 1, \\ 0, & \text{otherwise.} \end{cases}$$

where k is a constant. Find the value of k and determine $E(X)$ and $Var(X)$.

A is the event $X > \frac{1}{2}$, B is the event $X > \frac{3}{4}$.

Find:

(a) $P(B)$ (b) $P(B|A)$

25 A process for making plate glass produces small bubbles (imperfections) scattered at random in the glass, at an average rate of four small bubbles per $10\,m^2$.

Assuming a Poisson model for the number of small bubbles, determine, to 3 decimal places, the probability that a piece of glass $2.2\,m \times 3.0\,m$ will contain

(a) exactly two small bubbles

(b) at least one small bubble

(c) at most two small bubbles.

Show that the probability that five pieces of glass, each $2.5\,m \times 2.0\,m$, will all be free of small bubbles is e^{-10}.

Find, to 3 decimal places, the probability that five pieces of glass, each $2.5\,m \times 2.0\,m$, will contain a total of at least ten small bubbles. [E]

26 In the manufacture of a particular curtain material, small faults occur at random at an average of 0.85 per $10\,m^2$.

(a) Find the probability that in a randomly selected $40\,m^2$ area of this material there are at most 2 faults.

This curtain material is going to be used in 10 of the rooms of a small block of furnished flats. Each room will require $40\,m^2$ of the material.

(b) Find the probability that for the first room to be furnished the material will contain at least 1 fault.

(c) Find the probability that in exactly half of these 10 rooms the material will contain exactly 3 faults.

The hooks on which these curtains are to hang are produced by a company that claims that only 2% of the hooks it produces are defective. The owner of the block of flats buys 500 of the hooks that have been selected at random from the production.

(d) Using a suitable approximation find the probability that this sample contains between 8 and 12 defective hooks, inclusive. [E]

27 A large store sells a certain size of nail either in a small packet at 50p per packet, or loose at £3 per kg. On any shopping day the number, X, of packets sold is a random variable where $X \sim B(8, 0.6)$, and the weight, Y kg, of nails

sold loose is a continuous random variable with probability density function f(y) given by

$$f(y) = \begin{cases} \dfrac{2(y-1)}{25}, & 1 \leqslant y \leqslant 6, \\ 0, & \text{otherwise.} \end{cases}$$

Find, to 3 decimal places, the probability that, on any shopping day, the number of packets sold will be:

(a) more than one   (b) seven or fewer.

Find the probability that:

(c) the weight of nails sold loose on any shopping day will be between 4 kg and 5 kg,

(d) on any one shopping day the shop will sell exactly 2 packets of nails and less than 2 kg of nails sold loose, giving your answer to 2 significant figures.

(e) Calculate the expected money received on any shopping day from the sale of this size of nail in this store.   [E]

28 A teacher of young children is thinking of asking her class to guess her height in metres. The teacher considers that the height guessed by a randomly selected child can be modelled by the random variable H with probability density function

$$f(h) = \begin{cases} \tfrac{3}{16}(4h - h^2), & 0 \leqslant h \leqslant 2, \\ 0, & \text{otherwise.} \end{cases}$$

Using this model,

(a) find $P(H < 1)$

(b) show that $E(H) = 1.25$.

A friend of the teacher suggests that the random variable X with probability density function

$$g(x) = \begin{cases} kx^3, & 0 \leqslant x \leqslant 2, \\ 0, & \text{otherwise.} \end{cases}$$

where k is a constant, might be a more suitable model.

(c) Show that $k = \tfrac{1}{4}$.

(d) Find $P(X < 1)$.

(e) Find $E(X)$.

(f) Using your calculations in (a), (b), (d) and (e), state, giving reasons, which of the random variables H or X is likely to be the more appropriate model in this instance.   [E]

29 The probability density function f(x) of a continuous random variable X is given by

$$f(x) = \begin{cases} kx^2(2 - x), & \text{for } 0 \leqslant x \leqslant 2, \\ 0, & \text{elsewhere.} \end{cases}$$

where k is a constant.

(a) Evaluate k.

(b) Draw a sketch of f(x), giving the x-coordinate of the maximum point.

(c) Calculate P($1 \leqslant X \leqslant 2$).

(d) Find the mean and variance of X.

30 The number, X, of breakdowns per day of the lifts in a large block of flats has a Poisson distribution with mean 0.2. Find, to 3 decimal places, the probability that on a particular day:

(a) there will be at least one breakdown

(b) there will be at most two breakdowns.

Find, to 3 decimal places, the probability that, during a 20 day period, there will be no lift breakdowns.   [E]

31 A new headache cure stops headaches completely for three out of five sufferers. What is the probability that when the cure is given to 4 sufferers 3 of them will be completely cured?

32 The random variable $X \sim B(10, 0.2)$. Find P($X \leqslant 3$).

33 The random variable M is B(20, 0.35). Find P($M \leqslant 12$).

34 Scrummy-biscs manufactures biscuits which are packed at random in presentation boxes, each box containing 20 biscuits. The company produces 45% chocolate biscuits, the remainder being plain biscuits. Five per cent of all the biscuits made are wrapped in coloured foil.

A box is selected at random from the production line. The random variable C represents the number of chocolate biscuits contained in this box.

(a) Write down two reasons to support the use of the binomial distribution as a suitable model for the random variable C.

(b) Calculate the probability that this box contains

(i) exactly 8 chocolate biscuits

(ii) more chocolate biscuits than plain biscuits.

35 Telephone calls arriving at a company switchboard are referred immediately, by the receptionist, to other people in the company. The duration of a call, in minutes, is modelled by a continuous random variable T, having probability density function

$$f(t) = \begin{cases} kt, & 0 \leqslant t \leqslant 15, \\ 0, & \text{otherwise.} \end{cases}$$

(a) Find the value of k.

(b) Find the cumulative distribution of T and specify it for all values of t.

(c) Find the probability that the duration of a telephone call is between 10 and 12 minutes.

(d) Sketch the form of the probability density function.

Suppose you have observations of the length of telephone calls to the switchboard and became convinced that the model was inappropriate.

(e) Sketch the shape of a probability density function which you might feel to be more realistic. [E]

36 Based on past experience, the manager of a telephone switchboard thinks that the number of telephone calls received in half-minute intervals can be modelled by a Poisson distribution with mean 3.5 calls per half-minute.

(a) Find the probability that at least 2 calls will be received by the switchboard in a randomly chosen half-minute interval.

(b) Find the probability that 5 or fewer calls will be received in a randomly chosen one-minute interval.

The manager decides to refine the Poisson model by monitoring the number of telephone calls, x, received by the switchboard in 90 successive half-minute intervals. The results are summarised as follows:

$$\sum x = 333, \quad \sum x^2 = 1562$$

(c) Calculate the mean and the variance of the number of calls received in the 90 half-minute intervals.

(d) Explain how your answers from part (c) support the choice of a Poisson model.

(e) Using the refined model, estimate the probability that exactly 3 calls will be received at the exchange in a randomly chosen half-minute interval. [E]

Continuous distributions

3

3.1 The continuous uniform (rectangular) distribution

If you are asked 'How tall are you?', you might respond 'I am 6 feet 1 inch tall'. By this you would *not* mean that you are exactly 6 feet 1 inch, or 73 inches, tall but that your height is between $72\frac{1}{2}$ inches and $73\frac{1}{2}$ inches and that it is equally likely to be anywhere in that range. What has happened is that your height is recorded to the nearest inch and the difference between your true height and your recorded height is a quantity that is equally likely to take any value between -0.5 inch and $+0.5$ inch. If all the students in your statistics group recorded their heights to the nearest inch then a reasonable model for the rounding errors produced is the continuous uniform distribution on the interval $(-0.5\ 0.5)$. If you let X represent the rounding errors then a sketch of the p.d.f. of X is as shown below.

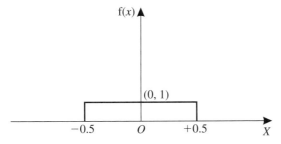

Note that the area under the p.d.f. is equal to unity and thus for this situation:

$$f(x) = 1 \qquad -0.5 \leqslant x \leqslant 0.5$$

It is useful to draw a sketch of any p.d.f. since it will often give you an insight into the shape of the distribution and perhaps more importantly the parameters of the distribution. For example, you can see from the above sketch, that the distribution is symmetrical about the zero, so the mean and median are both zero and that the distribution does not have a mode.

Generalising the above for a random variable X, having a continuous uniform distribution over the interval (α, β) gives:

$$f(x) = \begin{cases} \dfrac{1}{\beta - \alpha}, & \alpha < x < \beta, \\ 0, & \text{otherwise.} \end{cases}$$

A sketch of the p.d.f. is as follows:

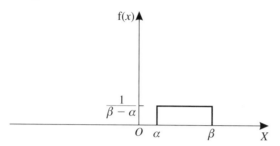

The geometry of the sketch shows that $f(x)$ is a valid p.d.f., since the area under the p.d.f. is given by:

$$\frac{1}{\beta - \alpha} \times (\beta - \alpha) = 1$$

Alternatively:

$$\int_\alpha^\beta \frac{1}{\beta - \alpha} \, \mathrm{d}x = \left(\frac{x}{\beta - \alpha} \right)_\alpha^\beta$$

$$= \frac{\beta - \alpha}{\beta - \alpha}$$

$$= 1$$

By symmetry:

$$\text{the mean} = \text{median} = \frac{\alpha + \beta}{2}$$

but if you are unsure about these values, use the definitions given earlier in the book, together with your knowledge of calculus, to verify them.

The variance of the distribution is found using:

$$\mathrm{Var}(X) = \mathrm{E}(X^2) - \{\mathrm{E}(X)\}^2$$

$$E(X^2) = \int_\alpha^\beta \frac{x^2}{(\beta - \alpha)} \, \mathrm{d}x$$

$$= \frac{1}{\beta - \alpha} \left(\frac{x^3}{3} \right)_\alpha^\beta$$

$$= \frac{\beta^3 - \alpha^3}{3(\beta - \alpha)}$$

$$= \frac{\beta^2 + \alpha\beta + \alpha^2}{3}$$

$\therefore \qquad \mathrm{Var}(X) = \frac{1}{3}(\beta^2 + \alpha\beta + \alpha^2) - \frac{1}{4}(\alpha + \beta)^2$

$\qquad\qquad\quad = \frac{1}{12}\{4\beta^2 + 4\alpha\beta + 4\alpha^2 - 3\alpha^2 - 6\alpha\beta - 3\beta^2\}$

$\qquad\qquad\quad = \frac{1}{12}\{\beta^2 - 2\alpha\beta + \alpha^2\}$

$\qquad\qquad\quad = \frac{1}{12}(\beta - \alpha)^2$

Sometimes it is advantageous to know the cumulative distribution function for a random variable and for X as defined above:

$$F(x_0) = P(X \leqslant x_0)$$

$$= \int_\alpha^{x_0} \frac{1}{\beta - \alpha}\,\mathrm{d}x$$

$$= \left(\frac{x}{\beta - \alpha}\right)_\alpha^{x_0}$$

$$= \frac{x_0 - \alpha}{\beta - \alpha} \qquad \alpha < x_0 < \beta$$

Example 1

The continuous variable X is uniformly distributed over the interval (2,5). Find:

(a) $\mathrm{E}(X)$ \qquad (b) $\mathrm{Var}(X)$ \qquad (c) $P(X > 3.8)$.

A sketch of the p.d.f. of x is as shown below

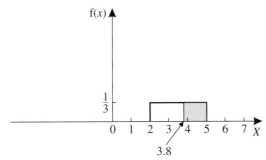

(a) $\mathrm{E}(X) = 3.5$ \qquad by symmetry

$\qquad$ or $\qquad\qquad\qquad \mathrm{E}(X) = \int_2^5 x\frac{1}{3}\,\mathrm{d}x$

$$= \frac{1}{3}\left(\frac{x^2}{2}\right)_2^5$$

$$= \frac{1}{3}\left(\frac{25}{2} - \frac{4}{2}\right)$$

$$= \frac{1}{3} \times \frac{21}{2}$$

$$= \frac{7}{2}$$

$$= 3.5$$

(b)
$$\mathrm{Var}(X) = \mathrm{E}(X^2) - \{\mathrm{E}(X)\}^2$$
$$= \tfrac{1}{12}(\beta - \alpha)^2$$

In this case $\beta = 5$ and $\alpha = 2$

$$\therefore \qquad \mathrm{Var}(X) = \tfrac{1}{12}(5-2)^2$$
$$= \tfrac{9}{12}$$
$$= \tfrac{3}{4}$$

Although the Edexcel booklet of mathematical formulae contains the formulae for the mean and variance of the continuous uniform distribution – often known as the **rectangular distribution** – it is important that you can obtain answers from first principles as well as from given formulae. Now show that
$$\mathrm{Var}(X) = \tfrac{3}{4} \text{ using } \mathrm{Var}(X) = \mathrm{E}(X^2) - \{\mathrm{E}(X)\}^2.$$

(c)
$$\mathrm{P}(X > 3.8) = \int_{3.8}^{5} \mathrm{f}(x)\,\mathrm{d}x$$
$$= \int_{3.8}^{5} \tfrac{1}{3}\,\mathrm{d}x$$
$$= \tfrac{1}{3}(x)_{3.8}^{5}$$
$$= \frac{5 - 3.8}{3}$$
$$= \frac{1.2}{3}$$
$$= 0.4$$

or $\mathrm{P}(X > 3.8) = 1 - \mathrm{F}(3.8)$
$$= 1 - \left(\frac{3.8 - 2}{5 - 2}\right)$$
$$= 1 - \frac{1.8}{3}$$
$$= \frac{1.2}{3}$$
$$= 0.4$$

or $\mathrm{P}(X > 3.8) = $ shaded area shown in sketch
$$= \tfrac{1}{3}(5 - 3.8)$$
$$= \frac{1.2}{3}$$
$$= 0.4$$

Example 2

A piece of string of length 8 cm is randomly cut into two pieces. Find the probability that the longer of the two pieces of string is at least 5 cm long.

Let X represent the distance of the cut from one end of the piece of string. Thus X has a uniform distribution over the interval $(0,8)$ and the p.d.f. of X is illustrated below.

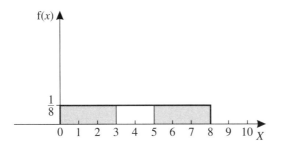

The longer piece of string is at least 5 cm long if $0 \leqslant X \leqslant 3$ or $5 \leqslant X \leqslant 8$. Since these intervals are mutually exclusive

$$P(0 \leqslant X \leqslant 3 \text{ or } 5 \leqslant X \leqslant 8) = P(0 \leqslant X \leqslant 3) + P(5 \leqslant X \leqslant 8)$$

$$= \frac{3-0}{8-0} + \frac{8-5}{8-0}$$

$$= \tfrac{3}{8} + \tfrac{3}{8}$$

$$= \tfrac{3}{4}$$

Exercise 3A

1 Find $E(X)$ and $Var(X)$ for the continuous random variable X having the following probability density functions:

(a) $f(x) = \begin{cases} \frac{1}{10}, & 10 \leqslant x \leqslant 20, \\ 0, & \text{otherwise.} \end{cases}$

(b) $f(x) = \begin{cases} \frac{1}{6}, & -3 \leqslant x \leqslant 3, \\ 0, & \text{otherwise.} \end{cases}$

(c) $f(x) = \begin{cases} \frac{1}{3}, & -1 \leqslant x \leqslant 2, \\ 0, & \text{otherwise.} \end{cases}$

2 For the random variable X, whose probability density function is shown below, find, using first principles, $E(X)$, $Var(X)$ and $P(X > 5.5)$.

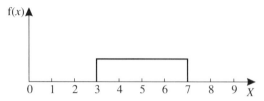

3 A clock stops at random. The random variable X is the hour as indicated by the hour hand.

(a) Write down the probability density function which describes X, and sketch its graph.

(b) Find the probability that the hand is between 3 o'clock and 7 o'clock.

4 A uniform steel bar was loaded until it broke. The loaded length of bar was 240 mm.

(a) Find the probability that the break did not lie in the middle third of the bar.

(b) If x is the distance in from the end of the bar at which it broke, find $E(X)$ and $Var(X)$.

5 A continuous random variable Y is uniformly distributed. Given that $E(Y) = 3$ and $Var(Y) = 3$, find $P(Y < 2)$.

6 The continuous random variable X is uniformly distributed over the interval (1,6).

(a) Find $E(X)$ and $Var(X)$.

(b) Write down the cumulative distribution function for X and use it to find $P(X < 4)$.

3.2 The normal distribution as an approximation to the binomial distribution

Earlier in the book you were introduced to two important discrete probability distributions – the binomial distribution and the Poisson distribution. Let us consider the discrete random variable having a binomial distribution, such that $X \sim B(n, p)$, where n represents the fixed number of trials used and p the constant probability of success at any trial. If, for example, $n = 10$ and $p = 0.3$, then you can evaluate probabilities associated with $X \sim B(10, 0.3)$ either from tables or using the distribution itself. Thus:

$$P(X = 1) = \binom{10}{1}(0.3)^1(0.7)^9$$

$$= 0.1211 \qquad \text{using your calculator}$$

$$\text{or } P(X \leqslant 7) = 0.9984 \qquad \text{from tables.}$$

When n becomes large, say 75, tabular values are not available and calculations become tedious. In such situations it is possible to use the normal distribution to find approximate values for the binomial probabilities and, provided you keep to the guidelines associated with the normal approximation to the binomial, then the approximations are reasonably accurate.

It is important to remember that the binomial distribution is used with *discrete* random variables and the normal distribution with *continuous* random variables. Hence we are approximating a discrete random variable by a continuous one and an allowance must be made for this using the $\frac{1}{2}$ **continuity correction**, as follows:

Let $X \sim B(100, 0.3)$, so that X can only take integer values $0, 1, ..., 100$, and in particular consider $x = 52$. Since X is discrete, $P(X = 52)$ can be found. However, when finding probabilities using continuous random variables it is not possible to find exact probabilities such as $P(X = 52)$, we have to find probabilities using the area under the p.d.f. between two given values. Referring back to the example on height at the beginning of section 3.1, a height of 73 inches was interpreted to range from $72\frac{1}{2}$ inches to $73\frac{1}{2}$ inches. Similarly, in situations where a discrete variable is being approximated by a continuous one, discrete values are converted into continuous ones by using the $\frac{1}{2}$ as illustrated with height. Hence, the name '$\frac{1}{2}$ continuity correction'. Thus, $P(X = 52)$ is approximated by $P(51\frac{1}{2} < Y < 52\frac{1}{2})$ where Y is a normal random variable. But what are the parameters of Y? Earlier in this book, the mean and variance of X when $X \sim B(n, p)$ were derived as $E(X) = np$, $Var(X) = np(1 - p)$. Thus when approximating a binomial distribution by a normal distribution np and $np(1 - p)$ are used as the mean and variance for the normal distribution.

Thus, $X \sim B(n, p)$ is approximated by $Y \sim N(np, np(1 - p))$ and in particular, if $X \sim B(100, 0.3)$ then it is approximated using $Y \sim N(30, 21)$. In practice, another rule-of-thumb is needed for using the normal approximation to the binomial and the following is recommended:

$X \sim B(n, p)$ can be approximated by

$$Y \sim N(\mu, \sigma^2) \qquad \text{where } \mu = np, \sigma^2 = np(1 - p)$$

provided that n is large and $np > 5$ and $n(1 - p) > 5$.

Before evaluating a specific example it is essential that you understand how the $\frac{1}{2}$ continuity correction is applied. The diagram below should help you.

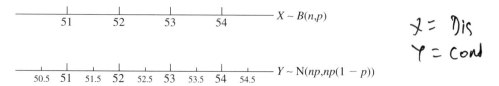

Hence we can approximate as follows:

$$P(X < 52) \simeq P(Y < 51\tfrac{1}{2})$$
$$P(X \leqslant 52) \simeq P(Y < 52\tfrac{1}{2})$$
$$P(X > 54) \simeq P(Y > 54\tfrac{1}{2})$$
$$P(X \geqslant 54) \simeq P(Y > 53\tfrac{1}{2})$$
$$P(52 < X < 54) \simeq P(52\tfrac{1}{2} < Y < 53\tfrac{1}{2})$$
$$P(52 \leqslant X < 54) \simeq P(51\tfrac{1}{2} < Y < 53\tfrac{1}{2})$$
$$P(52 \leqslant X \leqslant 54) \simeq P(51\tfrac{1}{2} < Y < 54\tfrac{1}{2})$$

$X = \text{Dis}$
$Y = \text{Cont}$

$P(X < \alpha) \simeq P(Y < \alpha - \tfrac{1}{2})$
$P(X \leqslant \alpha) \simeq P(Y < \alpha + \tfrac{1}{2})$
$P(X > \alpha) \simeq P(Y > \alpha + \tfrac{1}{2})$
$P(X \geqslant \alpha) \simeq P(Y > \alpha - \tfrac{1}{2})$

$P(\alpha \leqslant X \leqslant \beta)$
$P(\alpha - \tfrac{1}{2} < X \leqslant \beta + \tfrac{1}{2})$

Example 3

If $X \sim B(100, 0.3)$, find $P(33 \leqslant X < 37)$.

For the distribution of X,

$$E(X) = np$$
$$= 100 \times 0.3$$
$$= 30$$

and
$$Var(X) = np(1 - p)$$
$$= 100 \times 0.3 \times 0.7$$
$$= 21$$

Since $n = 100$ and both np and $n(1 - p)$ exceed 5, you can use the normal approximation.

$\therefore \quad P(33 \leqslant X < 37) \simeq P(32.5 < Y < 36.5)$ where $Y \sim N(30, 21)$

$$= P\left(\frac{32.5 - 30}{\sqrt{21}} < Z < \frac{36.5 - 30}{\sqrt{21}}\right)$$
$$= P(0.55 < Z < 1.42)$$
$$= \Phi(1.42) - \Phi(0.55)$$
$$= 0.9222 - 0.7088$$
$$= 0.2314$$

Example 4
If $X \sim B(100, 0.3)$, find $P(X = 33)$ using:
(a) the binomial distribution
(b) the normal approximation.

Calculate the error in approximating.

(a) $P(X = 33) = \binom{100}{33}(0.3)^{33}(0.7)^{67}$

$= 0.0685$ using a calculator.

(b) $P(X = 33) \simeq P(32\frac{1}{2} < Y < 33\frac{1}{2})$ where $Y \sim N(30, 21)$

$= P(0.5455 < Z < 0.7638)$

$= \Phi(0.76) - \Phi(0.55)$ or $\Phi(0.7638) - \Phi(0.5455)$

$= 0.7764 - 0.7088$ $0.7775 - 0.7073$

$= 0.0676$ 0.0702

Error $= 0.0676 - 0.0685$ $0.0702 - 0.0685$

$= -0.0009$ -0.0017 with interpolation

As was mentioned in S1, there is no need to interpolate in the S2 examination but both answers are given for completeness.

3.3 The normal distribution as an approximation to the Poisson distribution

In a similar way it is possible to approximate the Poisson distribution using the normal distribution. In Chapter 1, a random variable X was defined to have a Poisson distribution with parameter λ if it had the probability function:

$$P(X = r) = \frac{e^{-\lambda}\lambda^r}{r!} \qquad r = 0, 1, 2, 3...$$

The mean and variance of X were given as $E(X) = \lambda$ and $Var(X) = \lambda$. Cumulative Poisson probabilities have been tabulated in the EDEXCEL tables for values of λ in the range $(0.5, 10)$ but if $\lambda > 10$ there are no tabular values and an approximation has to be used. Thus $X \sim Po(\lambda)$ can be approximated by $Y \sim N(\lambda, \lambda)$ and for values of $\lambda > 10$ the approximation is good. Again when using the normal approximation to the Poisson distribution the continuity correction must be incorporated.

Example 5

If $X \sim \text{Po}(22)$, find $P(X = 18)$ using:

(a) the Poisson distribution

(b) the normal approximation.

(a)
$$X \sim \text{Po}(22) \Rightarrow P(X = r)$$

$$= \frac{e^{-22} 22^r}{r!}$$

$$\therefore \qquad P(X = 18) = \frac{e^{-22} 22^{18}}{18!} = 0.0635$$

(b) $P(X = 18) \simeq P(17.5 < Y < 18.5)$ where $Y \sim N(22, 22)$

$$= P\left(\frac{17.5 - 22}{\sqrt{22}} < Z < \frac{18.5 - 22}{\sqrt{22}}\right)$$

$$= P(-0.9594 < Z < -0.7462)$$

$$= \Phi(0.96) - \Phi(0.75) \qquad \text{or} \qquad \Phi(0.9594) - \Phi(0.7462)$$

$$= 0.8315 - 0.7734 \qquad\qquad 0.8313 - 0.7723$$

$$= 0.0581 \qquad\qquad 0.0590 \text{ with interpolation}$$

$$\text{Error} = 0.0581 - 0.0635 \qquad\qquad 0.0590 - 0.0635$$

$$= -0.0054 \qquad\qquad -0.0045 \text{ with interpolation}$$

Example 6

A car hire firm has a large fleet of cars for hire by the day and it is found that the fleet suffers breakdowns at the rate of 21 per week. Assuming that breakdowns occur at a constant rate, at random in time and independently of one another, calculate the probability that in any one week more than 27 breakdowns occur.

Let X represent the number of breakdowns per week.

$$\therefore X \sim \text{Po}(21)$$

$$\therefore \quad P(X > 27) \simeq P(Y > 27.5) \qquad \text{where } Y \sim N(21, 21)$$

$$= P\left(Z > \frac{27.5 - 21}{\sqrt{21}}\right)$$

$$= P(Z > 1.42) \qquad \text{or} \qquad P(Z > 1.4184)$$

$$= 1 - \Phi(1.42) \qquad\qquad 1 - \Phi(1.4184)$$

$$= 1 - 0.9222 \qquad\qquad 1 - 0.9220$$

$$= 0.0778 \qquad\qquad 0.0780 \text{ with interpolation}$$

Exercise 3B

1 Let $X \sim B(n, p)$ and $Y \sim N(np, np(1 - p))$. For each of the following probabilities in X, write the corresponding probability in Y when using a normal approximation:
   (a) $P(X < 26)$ (b) $P(X \leqslant 41)$ (c) $P(X > 10)$
   (d) $P(X \geqslant 5)$ (e) $P(2 \leqslant X < 10)$ (f) $P(40 < X \leqslant 50)$

2 Let $X \sim Po(\lambda)$ and $Y \sim N(\lambda, \lambda)$. For each of the following probabilities in X, write the corresponding probability in Y when using a normal approximation.
   (a) $P(X > 32)$ (b) $P(X \leqslant 16)$ (c) $P(X \geqslant 9)$
   (d) $P(X < 48)$ (e) $P(24 \leqslant X \leqslant 36)$ (f) $P(4 < X < 10)$

3 Which of the following could reasonably be approximated by a normal distribution?
   (a) $X \sim B(50, 0.3)$ (b) $Y \sim B(12, 0.4)$ (c) $X \sim B(15, 0.4)$
   (d) $Y \sim Po(8)$ (e) $X \sim Po(28)$

4 Use a normal approximation to find:
   (a) $P(X < 44)$ if $X \sim B(100, 0.5)$
   (b) $P(X \geqslant 60)$ if $X \sim B(80, 0.6)$
   (c) $P(X = 35)$ if $X \sim B(80, 0.4)$
   (d) $P(20 < X \leqslant 25)$ if $X \sim B(60, 0.3)$

5 Use a normal approximation to find:
   (a) $P(Y < 4)$ if $Y \sim Po(12)$
   (b) $P(Y \geqslant 15)$ if $Y \sim Po(22)$
   (c) $P(Y = 36)$ if $Y \sim Po(42)$
   (d) $P(45 < Y \leqslant 65)$ if $Y \sim Po(60)$

6 For $Y \sim B(20, 0.4)$ find $P(3 < Y < 13)$
   (a) using tables
   (b) using a normal approximation.
   State the error in (b).

7 For $X \sim Po(10)$ find $P(6 < X < 16)$
   (a) using tables
   (b) using a normal approximation.
   State the error in (b).

8 Explain briefly the circumstances under which a normal distribution may be used as an approximation to a binomial distribution.
   Write down the mean and the variance of the Normal approximation to the binomial distribution $B(n, p)$.

In a multiple-choice examination, candidate Jones picks his answer to each question at random from the list of 3 answers provided, of which only one is correct. A candidate answering 18 or more questions correctly passes the examination.

(a) For a paper containing 45 questions, use a normal approximation to find, to 3 decimal places, the probability that Jones passes.

(b) It is required that the probability that Jones passes should be less than 0.005. Use a normal approximation to show that the paper should contain at most 31 questions. [E]

9 In the production of compact discs at a certain factory, the proportion of faulty discs is known to be $\frac{1}{5}$. Each week the factory produces 2000 discs. Estimate, to 2 significant figures, the probability that there will be at most 349 faulty discs produced in one week.

It costs 60p to produce a disc. A faulty disc has to be discarded, while a non-faulty disc is sold for £9. Find the expected profit made by the factory per week. [E]

10 State the conditions under which a normal distribution may be used as an approximation to the distribution $B(n, p)$, and write down, in terms of n and p, the mean and the variance of this normal approximation.

(a) A large bag of seeds contains three varieties in the ratios 4 : 2 : 1 and their germination rates are 50%, 60% and 80% respectively. Show that the probability that a seed chosen at random from the bag will germinate is $\frac{4}{7}$.

(b) Given that 150 seeds are chosen at random from the bag, estimate, to 3 decimal places, the probability that less than 90 of them will germinate. [E]

11 The disintegration of a radioactive specimen is known to be at the rate of 14 counts per sec. Using the normal approximation for a Poisson distribution determine the probability that in any given second the counts will be:

(a) 20, 21 or 22   (b) greater than 10

(c) above 12 but less than 16.

12 A marina hires out boats on a daily basis. The mean number of boats hired per day is 15. Using the normal approximation for a Poisson distribution, find, for a period of 100 days:

(a) how often 5 or less boats are hired

(b) how often exactly 10 boats are hired

(c) on how many days they will have to turn customers away if the marina owns 20 boats.

13 Explain briefly the conditions under which a Poisson distribution may be approximated by a normal distribution. Give an example of the use of this approximation.

Street light failures in a town occur at an average rate of one every two days. Assuming that X, the number of street light failures per week, has a Poisson distribution, find to 3 decimal places, using the tables provided or otherwise, the probabilities that the number of street lights that will fail in a given week will be

(a) exactly 2   (b) less than 6.

(c) Using an appropriate distribution that approximates to that of X, find, to 3 decimal places, the probability that there will be fewer than 45 street light failures in 10 weeks.   [E]

SUMMARY OF KEY POINTS

1 A random variable X, having a continuous uniform distribution over the interval (α, β) has p.d.f.

$$f(x) = \begin{cases} \dfrac{1}{\beta - \alpha}, & \alpha < x < \beta, \\ 0, & \text{otherwise.} \end{cases}$$

2 For a random variable X, having a uniform distribution

$$E(X) = \frac{\alpha + \beta}{2}$$

$$\text{Var}(X) = \tfrac{1}{12}(\beta - \alpha)^2.$$

3 A random variable $X \sim B(n, p)$ can be approximated by $Y \sim N(\mu, \sigma^2)$ when $\mu = np$ and $\sigma^2 = np(1 - p) = nq$ provided that n is large, $np > 5$ and $n(1 - p) = nq > 5$.

4 A random variable $X \sim Po(\lambda)$ can be approximated by

$$Y \sim N(\lambda, \lambda) \qquad \text{for } \lambda > 10$$

Hypothesis tests

4

In chapter 1 of Book S1 we talked about mathematical models and in chapter 1 of this book we have met two models, the binomial and the Poisson distributions. Whenever a mathematical model is proposed it is very important to test it in order to see how well it works. This testing can be done using a **hypothesis test**, a vital tool of the statistician, and two simple tests will be dealt with in this chapter but first we must look at sampling and sampling statistics.

4.1 Populations and sampling

In Book S1 we defined different types of data using the terms quantative, qualitative, discrete and continuous. In this book we are going to define groups or collections of individuals as items. Let us now consider the heights of three students chosen at random from year 13 in a sixth form college. The students are John, Sandra and Tony and their heights, in inches, are 70 in, 64 in and 73 in. In statistical language the heights of John, Sandra and Tony are a *sample* of the heights of the *population* of year 13 students in the college. A **population** is a collection of individuals or items. You may be able to draw conclusions about a small population by considering each individual or item. For a large population you may not want to consider every individual. Instead you may draw conclusions about the whole population by considering a **sample** – a selection of individual members of the population. Notice that in statistics the word population refers to data in general and not just to people. So we can have a population of year 13 students, female cyclists, potatoes, two-inch nails, and so on.

In some situations a population may be of **finite** size. For example, the number of students in a sixth form college is finite because it is possible to give each student an individual number and know exactly how many students there are. In some situations we consider a population to be of **infinite** size as it is impossible for us to know exactly how many members there are in that population. Such an example might be the number of rabbits on the North Yorkshire moors – however hard we try it will not be possible to number them individually. A third type of population is of **countably infinite** size where we know that the population is infinite and we *can* count and number the individual members of that population. For example, the number of throws of a dice needed to obtain a six produces a countably infinite population. We may obtain a six on the first throw or the second or the twentieth, but we might need to go on throwing for ever.

In practice populations are often too large to work with the data on each member, although it might be argued that a population of year 13 students in a sixth form college does not fall into this category. In this case each student *could* be identified individually and observations or measurements could be taken on every one. Then the total number of measurements would be known and we would have taken a **census**.

Sampling units

In most situations, due to considerations of time and cost it is necessary to take observations or measurements from a selection of individual members of the population. These individual members are known as **sampling units**. For example, John, Sandra and Tony are three of the sampling units making up the population of year 13 students in the sixth form college. In some circumstances a sampling unit may contain several elements. For example, if the sampling unit is a household containing several individuals then each individual is known as a **sampling element**. However, if each sampling unit contains one and only one element (such as Sandra) then a sampling unit and an element from the population are identical. In this book we use the term sampling unit to refer to an individual member of the population.

Sampling frame

Once the sampling units within a population are individually named or numbered to form a list then this list of sampling units is known as a **sampling frame**. For example, the class register of all the students in year 13 at the sixth form college is a sampling frame. In this example the sampling frame and the population should be the same provided the class register is up to date and accurate.

In practice the sampling frame may not include all the sampling units in the population because it may not be possible to keep details of the population up to date. For example, if we specify individual voters as the sampling units a list of all registered voters could serve as the sampling frame. This frame, however, is unlikely to contain all the voters in the population as it is impossible to update the list daily. So it is important to note that many sampling frames will contain some inadequacies of this type, but usually the difference between the population and the sampling frame is small enough to allow the sample drawn from the sampling frame to represent the population.

A sampling frame can take a variety of forms – list, index, map, file, database – but whatever its form, how well a sampling frame covers a population and its accuracy are important as the sampling frame is the basis of any sample drawn.

Example 1

Give an example of each of the following types of population

(a) finite   (b) infinite   (c) countably infinite.

(a) The number of students enrolled in The University of Teesside Business School in academic year 1999/2000 is a finite population.

(b) The number of telephone calls made in a year throughout the world can be considered to be an infinite population.

(c) Toss a coin until a head appears and then count the number of times the coin was tossed. The number of times is a countably infinite population.

Example 2

Suggest possible sampling frames to enable samples to be obtained relating to:

(a) couples married in Cleveland in 1999
(b) fish caught at Scaling Dam in July 1999
(c) voting patterns in Devon.

(a) A possible sampling frame would be the list of marriages recorded by the Registrar in Cleveland in 1999.

(b) A list of anglers registered as having licences to fish on Scaling Dam in July 1999.

(c) The electoral register of voters in Devon would be a possible sampling frame.

4.2 Advantages and disadvantages of sampling

Section 4.1 introduced the terminology of sampling. This section looks at the advantages and disadvantages associated with sampling. First let us consider some of the advantages:

If it can be assumed that a population is infinite and well mixed then a sample will be *representative* of the whole population. Consider, for example, a large tank full of liquid known to contain millions of bacteria. It would be impossible to number the individual bacteria, but if the tank is well stirred and a sample of liquid is taken from it, then it would be reasonable to assume that the sample is representative of the liquid in the tank. The bacteria in the volume of liquid removed would represent the bacteria in the total volume of the tank, and conclusions drawn from the sample should also be true for the whole tank.

Sampling is generally *cheaper* than taking a census, although the cost per sampling unit studied will usually be greater than for a census. However, as sampling concentrates on gaining information about selected sampling units, then the *quality of information* gained about each sampling unit is often better.

Sampling is also advantageous in situations where testing items results in their destruction (for example, testing the lifetimes of light bulbs), and where checking every item on a production line makes the process uneconomical.

When using a sample rather than a census, data is generally more *readily available* for analysis and more quickly analysed.

Sampling also has some disadvantages:

One definition of statistics is that 'statistics is the process of decision making in the face of uncertainty'. The *uncertainty* associated with sampling can be looked upon as a disadvantage. This uncertainty can take two forms – natural variation and bias.

Natural variation is due to chance differences among the sampling units. These differences cannot be controlled or accounted for by the person taking the sample.

Bias can be defined as anything which occurs when taking a sample that prevents the sample from representing the population from which it is being taken. It can occur for a variety of reasons which are usually to do with the definition of the population or the method of selecting the sample. Bias can occur through:

■ *sampling from an incomplete sampling frame* – for example, a sample chosen from the telephone directory of a city cannot provide a good estimate of the proportion of the population of that city who smoke.

■ the introduction of *personal subjective choice* by the person taking the sample – for example, a child asked to take a random sample of shells from a beach may tend to choose the more eye-catching brightly coloured ones.

■ *non-response* where responses are only obtained from those who have a particular interest in the study being undertaken – for example, a postal questionnaire sent to motorists about the particular model of car they drive will be ignored by the majority. Those completing and returning it are likely to be those who have had a good experience of that model or a very poor experience of it.

- *substituting convenient sample units* when those required are not easily available – for example, a sample which necessitates visits to households. The interviewer takes the next-door or nearest available household if there is no reply at the one chosen to be part of the sample.

Whatever the reasons for the presence of bias, it is worth noting that bias cannot be reduced by increasing the sample size, as every sample unit is likely to misrepresent the population in the same way.

4.3 Collecting sample data

Any sample of data you use should be a true (unbiased) representation of the population from which it is being drawn. For the purposes of this book and the S2 syllabus we shall assume that data have been obtained by the method of **simple random sampling**. If a population contains N sampling units and you require a sample of n of them, then a simple random sample is one such that every possible sample of size n has the same chance of being selected. In practice this is achieved by giving every member of the population an equal chance of selection, and using some form of random process (such as random numbers) to make the selection.

Details of simple random sampling and other methods of sampling are given in Book S3.

Exercise 4A

1 For each of the following populations, state whether it is finite, infinite, or countably infinite:
    (a) the number of points at which a dart can enter a circular dart board
    (b) the number of items coming off a production line
    (c) the number of professional tennis players.

2 Suggest appropriate sampling units for populations associated with the following:
    (a) a library   (b) a garage   (c) a hospital.

3 A market research organisation wants to take a sample of:
    (a) students studying at the University of Teesside
    (b) owners of L-registered motor cars
    (c) professional golfers.
    Suggest a suitable sampling frame in each case.

4 A safety expert is interested in estimating the proportion of motor cars with illegal tyres. Discuss possible sampling units and sampling frames.

5 A factory manager wishes to investigate the life-time of batteries produced in the factory. A random sample of 25 batteries is taken every day for four consecutive weeks and each battery is tested to exhaustion. Comment on the advantages and disadvantages associated with this sampling scheme.

6 A forester wants to estimate for a large forest the total number of trees that have a trunk diameter exceeding 18 inches. A map of the forest is available. Discuss the problem of choosing appropriate sampling units and an appropriate frame.

4.4 The concept of a statistic and its sampling distribution

A small company is thinking of installing a new telephone system and wants to know whether or not it should change the number of lines it has. The company decides to examine the number of calls received during 5 minute periods in the morning. The number of calls in each 5 minute period over the course of a year will form a large **population** of values such as 5, 0, 3, 2, 12, etc. We can call the mean number of calls μ. But the company does not know the value of μ and it cannot afford the time or money to find it. We shall call μ a **population parameter**: that is, it is the mean of the *whole population*. Greek letters are usually used to denote population parameters. There may be several parameters of interest in the population; for example in this population we might also be interested in the standard deviation of the number of calls, σ.

Population of number of calls to the company in 5 minute periods

Although the company may not be able to find out the value of μ (or σ) it may wish to make **inferences** about it and this can be achieved by carrying out a **hypothesis test**.

Before the company can make a statement or inference about μ they will need to take a sample from the population. As was mentioned in section 4.3, the theory required in S2 assumes that a simple random sample of size n is used.

The populations will consist of numbers and so therefore will any samples, as a sample is simply a subset of the population. In order to help describe the population it is helpful to introduce the random variable X which, in this case, represents the number of calls made to the company in a 5 minute period during the morning. We can then define the random variables X_1, X_2 and X_3, to refer to the first, second and third members of the sample, respectively. As the members of the sample will always be numbers, it makes sense to refer to the ith member of the sample as a random variable X_i (you will recall from Book S1, chapter 8, that a random variable must always have a numerical value). If the first three 5 minute periods taken in a sample from this population contained 5, 0 and 3 calls respectively, then we would write $x_1 = 5$, $x_2 = 0$ and $x_3 = 3$ where x_i, is the ith member of the sample. This follows the convention in book S1 where lower case letters refer to particular values of a random variable which is represented by the upper case form of the letter.

Given a random variable, the first question you should ask is, what is its distribution? The random variable X_1 is simply a randomly selected member of the population, as indeed are all the X_i. So X_1, and each of the X_i will have the *same distribution as the population* from which the sample is taken. So in particular $E(X_i) = \mu$ (and $\text{Var}(X_i) = \sigma^2$) for every member of the sample. Since the sample you are dealing with is a simple random sample, each of the X_i will also be an *independent* random variable.

- **A simple random sample of size n consists of the observations X_1, X_2, X_3, . . . X_n from a population where the X_i**
  – are independent random variables
  – have the same distribution as the population.

It is usual practice to drop the term 'simple' and refer to such a sample as a **random sample**.

So how can you use the sample to make statements or inferences about the parameters of the population? The only sources of information available to you are the observations in the sample and you must use some function of the sample values to carry out this task. Such a function is called a **statistic**.

- **If X_1, X_2, X_3, . . . X_n is a random sample of size n from some population then a statistic T is a random variable consisting of any function of the X_i that involves no other quantities.**

There are certain statistics that were introduced in Book S1, namely

$$\bar{X} = \frac{\sum X}{n} \quad \text{and} \quad S^2 = \frac{\sum (X - \bar{X})^2}{n-1}$$

and these are particularly important statistics, as you will see in Book S3. It is worth stressing that a statistic should not be a function involving any unknown quantities and the function $\dfrac{\sum (X - \mu)^2}{n}$,

which was also introduced in book S1, is *not* a statistic as it involves the parameter μ, which is usually unknown.

Since it is possible to repeat the process of taking a sample, the particular value of a statistic Y in a specific case, namely y, will be different for each sample. If all possible samples are taken then these values will form a probability distribution called the **sampling distribution of Y**.

■ **The distribution of the X_i (which is the same as the distribution of the population) will determine the distribution of a statistic Y. This is called the sampling distribution of the statistic.**

In our example we can model the random variable X, representing the number of calls in a 5 minute period, with a Poisson distribution of mean μ. As we shall see in section 4.9, we would usually make inferences about μ based on a single observation so the statistic we should use is X_1 and its sampling distribution is $Po(\mu)$, i.e. a Poisson distribution with mean μ.

Example 3

A new political party is seeking to determine the degree of support it would have amongst the electorate. The random variable X is defined as:

$$X = \begin{cases} 1, & \text{if the voter would support the party,} \\ 0, & \text{otherwise.} \end{cases}$$

A random sample of 20 voters are presented with a simple summary of the party's policies and asked if they would vote for this new party. The random sample is represented by $X_1, X_2, \ldots, X_{20}$.

(a) Suggest a suitable population and identify any possible parameter of interest.
(b) Write down the sampling distribution of the statistic

$$Y = \sum_{i=1}^{20} X_i$$

(a) The population will be based upon the responses of the voters. In terms of the random variable X it will consist of a series of 1s and 0s depending whether an individual voter would or would not support the party. The parameter of interest is p, representing the proportion of 1s in the population.
(b) $Y =$ the number of voters who would support the party.

Since the sample is random (and therefore each observation is independent), p is constant and the responses are either success (1) or failure (0) then:

Y will have a binomial distribution with $n = 20$ and parameter p, i.e. $Y \sim B(20, p)$.

Example 4

A large bag contains counters. Sixty per cent of the counters have the number 0 on them and forty per cent have the number 1.
(a) Find the mean μ and variance σ^2 for this population of counters.
A simple random sample of size 3 is taken from this population.
(b) List all possible samples.
(c) Find the sampling distribution for the mean

$$\bar{X} = \frac{X_1 + X_2 + X_3}{3}$$

(d) Find the sampling distribution for the mode M.

(a) The distribution of the population is

$$X: \quad 0 \quad 1$$
$$P(X = x): \quad \tfrac{3}{5} \quad \tfrac{2}{5}$$

$$\mu = E(x) = \sum_{\forall x} xP(X = x) = 0 + \tfrac{2}{5} \Rightarrow \mu = \tfrac{2}{5}$$

$$\sigma^2 = \text{Var}(X) = \sum_{\forall x} x^2 P(X = x) - \mu^2 = 0 + 1^2 \cdot \tfrac{2}{5} - \tfrac{4}{25} \Rightarrow \sigma^2 = \tfrac{6}{25}$$

(b) The possible samples are

$$(0, 0, 0)$$
$$(1, 0, 0) \ (0, 1, 0) \ (0, 0, 1)$$
$$(1, 1, 0) \ (1, 0, 1) \ (0, 1, 1)$$
$$(1, 1, 1)$$

(c) $P(\bar{X} = 0) = \left(\tfrac{3}{5}\right)^3 = \tfrac{27}{125}$ i.e. the (0,0,0) case

$P(\bar{X} = \tfrac{1}{3}) = 3 \cdot \tfrac{2}{5} \cdot \left(\tfrac{3}{5}\right)^2 = \tfrac{54}{125}$ i.e. the (1,0,0); (0,1,0); (0,0,1) cases

$P(\bar{X} = \tfrac{2}{3}) = 3 \cdot \left(\tfrac{2}{5}\right)^2 \cdot \tfrac{3}{5} = \tfrac{36}{125}$ i.e. the (1,1,0); (1,0,1); (0,1,1) cases

$P(\bar{X} = 1) = \left(\tfrac{2}{5}\right)^3 = \tfrac{8}{125}$ i.e. the (1,1,1) case.

So the distribution for $\bar{X}$ is

$\bar{X}$:	0	$\tfrac{1}{3}$	$\tfrac{2}{3}$	1
p($\bar{x}$):	$\tfrac{27}{125}$	$\tfrac{54}{125}$	$\tfrac{36}{125}$	$\tfrac{8}{125}$

(d) The mode M can take values 0 or 1.

$$P(M = 0) = \tfrac{27}{125} + \tfrac{54}{125} = \tfrac{81}{125} \text{ [i.e. cases (0,0,0); (1,0,0); (0,1,0); (0,0,1)]}$$

and $P(M = 1) = \tfrac{44}{125}$ [i.e. the other cases]

so the distribution of M is

M:	0	1
p(m):	$\tfrac{81}{125}$	$\tfrac{44}{125}$

Exercise 4B

1 The weights of apples from a certain orchard are assumed to have mean μ and standard deviation σ. A sample of 30 apples was taken and their weights recorded. If the sample is represented by $X_1, X_2, \ldots X_{30}$ state whether or not the following are statistics.

(a) $\dfrac{X_1 + X_{30}}{2}$ ✓   (b) $\dfrac{\Sigma X}{30}$ (c) $\dfrac{\Sigma |X - \mu|}{30}$

(d) $\dfrac{\Sigma(X - \bar{X})^2}{30}$ (e) $\dfrac{\Sigma X^2}{30} - \sigma^2$ (f) $\Sigma \left(\dfrac{X - \mu}{\sigma} \right)$

(g) $\text{Max}\{X_1, X_2, X_3, \ldots X_{30}\}$ ✓

2 A machine produces components for an electrical appliance but 5% of these are defective. A random sample of 20 components are checked and the random variables $X_i : i = 1, 2, \ldots 20$ are defined as follows:

$$X_i = \begin{cases} 1, & \text{if the } i\text{th component is defective,} \\ 0, & \text{if the } i\text{th component is not defective.} \end{cases}$$

(a) Write down the distribution for ΣX_i, i.e. the total number of defectives in the sample.

(b) Find $P(\Sigma X_i \leqslant 2)$.

(c) Find $E(\Sigma X_i)$ and $\text{Var}(\Sigma X_i)$.

3 Repeat question 2 if the proportion that are defective is p.

4 A quarter of the pupils in a large school come to school by bus. A random sample of 10 pupils is selected and the random variables X_i are defined as follows

$$X_i = \begin{cases} 1, & \text{if the pupil comes to school by bus,} \\ 0, & \text{otherwise.} \end{cases}$$

(a) Write down the distribution for ΣX_i the total number of pupils in the sample who come to school by bus.

(b) Find $P(\Sigma X_i > 2)$ and $P(\Sigma X_i > 6)$.

(c) Find $E(\Sigma X_i)$ and $\text{Var}(\Sigma X_i)$.

5 A secretary makes mistakes at an average rate of 3 every 10 pages. She has just finished typing a 5 page document.

(a) Write down a suitable sampling distribution for the number of mistakes in this document.

(b) Find the probability that the document contains fewer than 2 mistakes.

6 The 'bran tub', filled with sawdust, at a village fair is supposed to contain 100 prizes. The tub holds 125 litres. A parent pays for three children to have a go, and between them they search through 1 litre of sawdust.

(a) Suggest a suitable model for the number of prizes per litre in the tub. State any assumptions required.

(b) Find the probability that the total number of prizes the children receive is at least 3.

Another family search through 2.5 litres of sawdust.

(c) Suggest a suitable sampling distribution for the number of prizes they find.

7 A large bag of coins contains 1p, 5p and 10p coins in the ratio 3 : 2 : 1.

(a) Find the mean μ and the variance σ^2 for the value of coins in this population.

A random sample of two coins is taken and their values X_1 and X_2 are recorded.

(b) List all possible samples.

(c) Find the sampling distribution for the mean $\bar{X} = \dfrac{X_1 + X_2}{2}$.

8 A manufacturer of self-assembly furniture required bolts of two lengths, 5 cm and 10 cm, in the ratio 3 : 1 respectively.

(a) Find the mean μ for the lengths of bolts in this population.

A random sample of three bolts is selected from a large box containing bolts in the required ratio.

(b) List all possible samples.

(c) Find the sampling distribution for the mean $\bar{X}$.

(d) Find the sampling distribution for the mode M.

9 A large bag of counters has 25% with the number 0 on, 25% with the number 2 on and 50% with the number 1.

(a) Find the mean μ for this population of counters.

A random sample of size 3 is taken from the bag.

(b) List all possible samples.

(c) Find the sampling distribution for the mean $\bar{X}$.

(d) Find the sampling distribution for the median N.

4.5 Concept and interpretation of a hypothesis test

The scene is a courtroom. The defendant is in the dock and is accused of committing murder. The prosecution and defence counsels will both present evidence and the judge and jury have to reach a verdict. Two important principles operate under the system of British law and they are:

1. the defendant is 'innocent until proved guilty'
2. the proof must be 'beyond all reasonable doubt'.

Clearly the defendant either did or did not commit the murder but, during the course of the trial, the assumption the judge and jury must make is that he did not (i.e. that he is innocent). They must then examine the evidence and essentially answer the following question:

If the defendant is innocent what is the probability
of obtaining the evidence presented?

If this probability is very small then they will conclude that the assumption of innocence is not sustainable and declare the defendant guilty. For example, if the defendant's fingerprints were found on the gun that shot the victim and the defendant was seen leaving the scene shortly after the time of death then you might think that the probability of these events happening and the defendant being innocent is quite small. Followers of TV detective programmes will know that it may well not be sufficiently small to secure a conviction though!

The above situation is very similar to the processes involved in carrying out a **hypothesis test**. The role of the defendant is played by the **hypotheses**. We start with a basic assumption called the **null hypothesis** (this is equivalent to the defendant being innocent), which is assumed to be true. We also specify the **alternative hypothesis** which describes the situation if the null hypothesis is not true (in the above situation it would be that the defendant was guilty and did commit the murder). In a statistical hypothesis test the evidence comes from a *sample*. This sample is summarised in the form of a statistic called a **test statistic** and by assuming the null hypothesis to be true it should be possible to calculate probabilities relating to this test statistic.

At this point another feature of the courtroom scenario is worth mentioning. Suppose that at the end of the trial the evidence presented is such that the judge and jury could decide that the defendant is guilty. Further evidence detrimental to the defendant could still be produced but a certain *threshold* has already been crossed. The probability of obtaining evidence as bad as this or worse is sufficiently small to cause the judge and jury to reject the defendant's innocence. The phrase **'as bad or worse'** is sometimes helpful. We calculate the probability of obtaining evidence *as bad or worse* as that which we have been presented with to make our judgement.

We said that the judge and jury must assess the evidence and attempt to estimate the probability of obtaining evidence 'as bad or worse' as that presented *if the defendant is innocent*. If that probability is very small they would reject the assumption of innocence, but how small is 'very small'? Clearly there is a *threshold* probability and it may vary, depending on the nature of the problem. In the context of a hypothesis test we call this threshold probability the **significance level**.

■ **If the probability of a value of the test statistic 'as bad or worse' as that obtained is p then we reject the null hypothesis if p is less than or equal to the significance level α.**

The significance level is the level of probability that we call *unlikely*. If your test gives a probability as unlikely as the significance level then you reject the null hypothesis. The usual significance level is 5% or 0.05 but other levels such as 1% (0.01) and 10% (0.10) are often used.

4.6 One and two-tailed tests

One rainy day during the summer holidays a family of four were playing a simple game of cards. The game was one of chance so the probability of any particular person winning should be $\frac{1}{4}$. After playing a number of games Robert complained that his younger sister Sarah must have been cheating as she kept winning. Their parents quickly intervened and decided to carry out a proper investigation.

Now Sarah may be cheating, but if she is not then the probability of her winning should be $\frac{1}{4}$, or the proportion, p, of games that Sarah wins is $\frac{1}{4}$. The test that the parents wish to carry out is about this proportion, p, of games that Sarah wins. It is a general feature of hypothesis tests that they are about *the value of unknown population parameters*. The defendant in this case is Sarah and her claim that $p = \frac{1}{4}$. We assume that Sarah is innocent and wish to formulate a null hypothesis to express this idea in terms of the parameter p. We usually write H_0 for the null hypothesis and in this case you have:

$$H_0 : p = \tfrac{1}{4}$$

If Sarah is guilty then the proportion of games that she wins must be more than $\frac{1}{4}$ (the complaint would probably not have arisen if she had not appeared to be winning more than her fair share of the games) and we write the alternative hypothesis, H_1, as

$$H_1 : p > \tfrac{1}{4}$$

This specification gives you a **one-tailed test**, since you are only considering deviations of p in one direction, namely $p > \frac{1}{4}$. Sarah's parents may have been interested in checking the hypothesis $p = \frac{1}{4}$ against the alternative hypothesis $p \neq \frac{1}{4}$. They could be concerned if she won very few games: maybe she had not understood the rules and this left her at a disadvantage, or she could be cheating and thus winning more games than expected. In this situation you would specify the alternative hypothesis as

$$H_1 : p \neq \frac{1}{4}$$

and this is called a **two-tailed test** since you are considering deviations of p in two directions.

Once the null and alternative hypotheses have been specified we need some procedure to decide between these two opposing hypotheses and the one that we use is called a **hypothesis test**.

■ **A hypothesis test about a population parameter θ tests a null hypothesis H_0, specifying a particular value for θ, against an alternative hypothesis H_1, which will indicate whether the test is one-tailed or two-tailed.**

The parents needed some evidence upon which to base their judgement and they examined a random sample of 10 games and discovered that Sarah had won 5 times. They then had to calculate the probability of obtaining evidence 'as bad or worse' than this, assuming that the null hypothesis is true. What sort of evidence would be 'as bad or worse' than that which their sample gave? The alternative hypothesis is that Sarah is cheating and that $p > \frac{1}{4}$; the sample saw Sarah winning 5 out of 10 games, a proportion of $\frac{1}{2}$, so if Sarah won 5 *or more* games that would constitute evidence 'as bad or worse'.

If we let the random variable X represent the number of times that Sarah wins in a sample of 10 games then, if the null hypothesis is true

$$X \sim \mathrm{B}(10, \tfrac{1}{4}).$$

The sample has given $x = 5$, so the required calculation is

$$
\begin{aligned}
\mathrm{P}(X \geqslant 5 | X \sim \mathrm{B}(10, \tfrac{1}{4})) &= 1 - \mathrm{P}(X \leqslant 4 | X \sim \mathrm{B}(10, \tfrac{1}{4})) \\
&= 1 - 0.9219 \text{ (using Table 1 on page 121)} \\
&= 0.0781
\end{aligned}
$$

The notation $\mathrm{P}(X \geqslant 5 | X \sim \mathrm{B}(10, 14))$ means the probability that $X \geqslant 5$ given that X has a binomial distribution with $n = 10$ and $p = \frac{1}{4}$. It is the same notation as was used for conditional probability in chapter 5 of book S1.

This probability (about 7.8%) is reasonably large (it is certainly more than 5%, which is the usual significance level) so there is no reason to suspect the validity of H_0 and Sarah remains innocent. We usually say that the sample is **not significant** and that there is insufficient evidence to reject the null hypothesis that $p = \frac{1}{4}$.

Notice that the test was based simply on the statistic X and this is the **test statistic** in this case. Its sampling distribution is the binomial distribution.

In this case it is certainly clear that Sarah has been quite lucky; 5 wins out of 10 is twice the number you might expect $(E(X) = np = 10 \times \frac{1}{4} = 2.5)$ but it is not *so* unusual that you would suspect foul play.

4.7 Critical region

It is sometimes helpful to consider what value x of the test statistic you would have needed before the parents might consider that Sarah was cheating. In other words, what value of x would provide sufficient evidence to reject the claim that $p = \frac{1}{4}$? If you use a 5% significance level then you require the value of c such that:

$$P(X \geqslant c) \leqslant 0.05 \quad \text{where } X \sim B(10, 0.25)$$

i.e. $\qquad 1 - P(X \leqslant c - 1) \leqslant 0.05$

i.e. $\qquad\quad P(X \leqslant c - 1) \geqslant 0.95$

Using Table 1 on page 121 we have

$$P(X \leqslant 4) = 0.9219$$

and $\qquad\qquad P(X \leqslant 5) = 0.9803$

thus when $c - 1 = 5$ or $c = 6$ we have $P(X \geqslant 6) = 0.0197$. So if Sarah had won 6 or more games out of the sample of 10 we would have had a **significant** result and rejected H_0. So any value $X \geqslant 6$ would mean that the probability of obtaining a sample 'as bad or worse' is less than or equal to 5%, which is unlikely. This means that the assumption that H_0 is true is called into question and we *reject H_0 at the 5% level of significance*. Notice that although we used a 5% level of significance, the probability of rejecting H_0 is only 0.0197, i.e. 1.97%, which is quite a bit less than the 5% we aimed for. This will often happen when our test statistic follows a discrete distribution, but when hypothesis tests are based on a continuous variable such as the normal distribution (as in S3) this situation will not arise.

We call the region $X \geqslant 6$ the **critical region** of the statistic X and the value 6 is called the **critical value**.

- **The critical region of a test statistic Y is the range of values of Y such that if the value of Y, namely y, obtained from your particular sample lies in this region then you reject the null hypothesis.**
- **The boundary value(s) of the critical region is (are) called the critical value(s).**

4.8 Hypothesis test for the proportion *p* of a binomial distribution

The standard treatment for a particular disease has a probability $\frac{2}{5}$ of success. A certain doctor has undertaken research in this area and has produced a new drug which has been successful with 11 out of 20 patients upon whom he has tested it. The doctor claims that the new drug represents an improvement on the standard treatment and is trying to sell his formula to a large drug company.

Is the doctor's claim justified? To answer this question you can set the problem up as a hypothesis test about the proportion *p* of the population of people with this disease for whom the drug is successful. The null hypothesis will be that $p = \frac{2}{5}$, that is, that there is no change, and the doctor's claim is that $p > \frac{2}{5}$. So you have:

$$H_0 : p = \tfrac{2}{5} \qquad H_1 : p > \tfrac{2}{5}$$

If the null hypothesis is true then the random variable X representing the number of patients for whom the new drug was successful has a $B(20, \frac{2}{5})$ distribution.

The value of X observed is $x = 11$ and values of X 'as bad or worse' would be $X \geqslant 11$ so the probability you need to calculate is

$$\begin{aligned} P(X \geqslant 11) &= 1 - P(X \leqslant 10) \\ &= 1 - 0.8725 \text{ (from Table 1)} \\ &= 0.1275 \end{aligned}$$

This probability is quite large (it is greater than 5%) and so you do not reject H_0.

The doctor might ask how many successful cases would be needed to obtain a significant result at the 5% level. To answer this question you need to find the critical values for the statistic X. Now you have

$$H_0 : p = \tfrac{2}{5} \qquad H_1 : p > \tfrac{2}{5}$$

so you want to find a value c so that

$$P(X \geqslant c) \leqslant 0.05$$

Table 1 at the back of this book gives values for $P(X \leqslant x)$, so you need to replace $P(X \geqslant c)$ by $1 - P(X \leqslant c - 1)$ to obtain

$$1 - P(X \leqslant c - 1) \leqslant 0.05$$

or
$$0.95 \leqslant P(X \leqslant c - 1)$$

Now Table 1 (with $n = 20$ and $p = 0.4$) gives:

$$P(X \leqslant 11) = 0.9435$$
$$P(X \leqslant 12) = 0.9790$$

so in this case you have $\qquad c - 1 = 12$

and therefore $\qquad\qquad\qquad c = 13$

So the doctor would need at least 13 cases to obtain significant evidence against H_0.

It is also worth pointing out that in this case, since the binomial distribution is *discrete* you have therefore had to round your critical value to the nearest appropriate integer.

Sometimes a two-tailed test may be required and the procedure is a simple extension of the one-tailed case.

Example 5

A psychologist is attempting to help a pupil improve his short-term memory. One of the tests the psychologist uses is to present the pupil with a tray of 10 objects and let him look at them for 1 minute before taking the tray away and asking the pupil to write down as many of the objects as he can. Over a period of several weeks the psychologist has ascertained that the proportion, p, of objects that the pupil remembers is 0.35. The pupil has just been on a long adventure holiday and the psychologist is interested to see if there has been any change in p. Find the critical values for a two-tailed test using a 5% significance level.

Let X represent the number of objects the pupil remembers.

$$H_0 : p = 0.35 \qquad H_1 : p \neq 0.35$$

Assuming H_0 is true then $X \sim B(10, 0.35)$.

For a two-tailed test at 5% level you require the values c_1 and c_2 so that

$$P(X \leqslant c_1) \leqslant 0.025 \quad \text{and} \quad P(X \geqslant c_2) \leqslant 0.025$$

From Table 1: $\qquad P(X \leqslant 0) = 0.0135$

and $\qquad\qquad P(X \leqslant 1) = 0.0860$

so the value of c_1 is 0.

Also: $\qquad P(X \geqslant 7) = 1 - P(X \leqslant 6) = 1 - 0.9740 = 0.0260$

and $\qquad P(X \geqslant 8) = 1 - P(X \leqslant 7) = 1 - 0.9952 = 0.0048$

so the value of c_2 is 8.

Thus the critical region for X is $X = 0$ or $X \geqslant 8$.

Because we are dealing with discrete distributions the values of X have to be taken to the nearest integer. This sometimes leads to awkward results, especially with two-tailed tests. If the value of p given by H_0 is not $\frac{1}{2}$ then the distribution of the test statistic X will not be symmetrical and the decision to choose the critical values to give a $2\frac{1}{2}\%$ rejection rate at each end can appear to be somewhat arbitrary. The final tests that result will usually not have a probability of rejecting H_0 equal to the significance level and this can mean that the level at which the test is *actually* being carried out can be quite different from the intended one.

In example 5

$$P(\text{rejecting } H_0) = P(X = 0|p = 0.35) + P(X \geqslant 8|p = 0.35)$$
$$= 0.0135 + 0.0048$$
$$= 0.0183$$

and this is not very close to the 5% significance level required. You will notice that if you included 7 in your critical region and defined the critical region for the test as:

$$X = 0 \text{ or } X \geqslant 7$$

then:

$$P(\text{rejecting } H_0) = P(X = 0|p = 0.35) + P(X \geqslant 7|p = 0.35)$$
$$= 0.0135 + 0.0260$$
$$= 0.0395$$

which is closer to the 5% significance level required.

It is usual practice, if a 5% two-tailed test is required, to use $2\frac{1}{2}\%$ at each end as given in example 5, but sometimes a slightly different critical region can be found if the test with the probability of rejecting H_0 as close as possible to 0.05 is required.

It is clear that these small-sample tests are somewhat crude and for ease of use they require tables of cumulative probabilities for the binomial distribution. In the S2 examination you could find some questions that require you to use the formula for the binomial distribution as the value for n or p is not included in the tables.

Exercise 4C

Carry out the following tests using the binomial distribution where the random variable X represents the number of successes.

1   $H_0: p = 0.25$; $H_1: p > 0.25$; $n = 10$, $x = 5$ and using a 5% level of significance

2   $H_0: p = 0.40$; $H_1: p < 0.40$; $n = 10$, $x = 1$ and using a 5% level of significance

3   $H_0: p = 0.30$; $H_1: p > 0.30$; $n = 20$, $x = 10$ and using a 5% level of significance

4 $H_0: p = 0.45$; $H_1: p < 0.45$; $n = 20$, $x = 3$ and using a 1% level of significance

5 $H_0: p = 0.50$; $H_1: p \neq 0.50$; $n = 20$, $x = 7$ and using a 10% level of significance

Find the critical regions for the test statistic X representing the number of successes for the following tests.

6 $H_0: p = 0.20$; $H_1: p > 0.20$; $n = 10$, using a 5% level of significance

7 $H_0: p = 0.15$; $H_1: p < 0.15$; $n = 20$, using a 5% level of significance

8 $H_0: p = 0.35$; $H_1: p > 0.35$; $n = 10$, using a 1% level of significance

9 $H_0: p = 0.40$; $H_1: p \neq 0.40$; $n = 20$, using a 5% level of significance

10 $H_0: p = 0.10$; $H_1: p > 0.10$; $n = 20$, using a 1% level of significance

11 The manufacturer of 'Supergold' margarine claims that people prefer this to butter. As part of an advertising campaign he asked five people to taste a sample of Supergold and a sample of butter and say which one they prefer. Four people chose Supergold. Assess the manufacturer's claim in the light of this evidence.

12 I tossed a coin 20 times and obtained a head on 6 occasions. Is there evidence that the coin is biased? Use a 5% two-tailed significance test.

13 A seed merchant usually keeps her stock in carefully monitored conditions. After the Christmas holidays one year she discovered that the monitoring system had broken down and there was a danger that the seed might have been damaged by frost. She decided to check a sample of 10 seeds to see if the proportion p that germinated had been reduced from the usual value of 0.85. Find the critical region for a one-tailed test using a 5% significance level.

14 A die used in playing a board game is suspected of not giving the number 6 often enough. During a particular game it was rolled 12 times and only 1 six appeared. Does this represent significant evidence that the probability of a six on this die is less than $\frac{1}{6}$?

15 'My research shows that 3 out of every 10 children say their favourite colour is red', announced the professor, but Miss Smith believed the proportion was much higher. She asked the group of 6 children in her after-school art club and 3 of them had red as their favourite colour. She uses a 5% level of significance.

(a) Test Miss Smith's belief on the basis of this sample.

She decided to ask a larger random sample of 20 children from the school playground at break the next day.

(b) Find how many children must choose red as their favourite colour for Miss Smith to have a significant result.

16 A new drug to stop asthma attacks is considered to be effective if an attack is completely relieved within 5 minutes. It is claimed that the drug is effective in 1 out of 6 attacks. Given that 8 sufferers are given the drug during an attack, find, to 3 decimal places, the probability that, if the claim is true,

(a) at least two   (b) less than three

of the sufferers will find the drug effective.

17 The success rate of the standard treatment for patients suffering from a particular skin disease is known to be 68%.

(a) In a sample of n patients, X is the number for which the treatment is successful. Write down a suitable distribution to model X. Give the reasons for your choice of distribution.

(b) A random sample of 10 patients receives the standard treatment. Find, to 3 decimal places, the probability that for exactly 6 patients the treatment will be successful.   [E]

18 Over a long period of time it has been found that in Enrico's restaurant the ratio of non-vegetarian to vegetarian meals ordered is 3 to 1.

During one particular day at Enrico's restaurant, a random sample of 20 people contained 2 who ordered a vegetarian meal. Carry out a significance test to determine whether or not the proportion of vegetarian meals ordered that day is lower than is usual. State clearly your hypotheses and use a 10% significance level.   [E]

4.9 Hypothesis test for the mean of a Poisson distribution

It is a simple extension to test for the mean of a Poisson distribution.

Example 6
Accidents used to occur at a certain road junction at a rate of 6 per month. The residents had petitioned for traffic lights but the planners believed that the average number of accidents per month could be reduced simply by erecting a warning sign. In the month following the erection of the warning sign there were only 3 accidents. Does this give sufficient evidence that the planners were correct? Use a 5% level of significance.

If you let the random variable X represent the number of accidents in a month and λ represent the average number of accidents per month, then you have observed $x = 3$ and hypotheses can be formulated in terms of λ as follows:

$$H_0 : \lambda = 6 \text{ (i.e. no change)} \qquad H_1 : \lambda < 6 \text{ (i.e. fewer accidents)}$$

Assuming that H_0 is true you require $P(X \leqslant 3)$ since evidence 'as bad or worse' for the null hypothesis will mean 3 or fewer accidents in a month.

From Table 2 (remembering that the parameter λ for a Poisson distribution is equal to the mean μ):

$$P(X \leqslant 3|\lambda = 6) = 0.1512$$

This is more than 5% so you do not reject H_0. The planners have not won their case and overturned the hypothesis that $\lambda = 6$.

In practice, of course, in a situation like this a much larger sample would probably be considered, say over a six-month period, and then the values of λ would be quite large and a normal approximation could be considered as in chapter 3.

As in the case of the tests for the proportion using a binomial distribution, you can formulate tests in terms of the critical region for the random variable X. In example 6 you can find the critical region for X as follows.

In order to reject H_0 the planners require a value c such that

$$P(X \leqslant c|\lambda = 6) \leqslant 0.05$$

From Table 2, with $\lambda = 6$:

$$P(X \leqslant 2) = 0.0620$$
and $$P(X \leqslant 1) = 0.0174$$

So the critical value c is 1 and the critical region for this test is $X \leqslant 1$. The probability that you reject H_0 when H_0 is true is simply 0.0174. This is much smaller than the 5% significance level that you were aiming for.

Exercise 4D

For each of questions 1–3 carry out the following tests. You may assume that the random variable X has a $\text{Po}(\lambda)$ distribution.

1 H_0: $\lambda = 8$; H_1: $\lambda < 8$; $x = 3$, using a 5% level of significance

2 H_0: $\lambda = 6.5$; H_1: $\lambda < 6.5$; $x = 2$, using a 1% level of significance

3 H_0: $\lambda = 5.5$; H_1: $\lambda > 5.5$; $x = 8$, using a 5% level of significance

For each of questions 4–6 find the critical region for the test statistic X given that X has a $\text{Po}(\lambda)$ distribution.

4 H_0: $\lambda = 4$; H_1: $\lambda > 4$; using a 5% level of significance

5 H_0: $\lambda = 9$; H_1: $\lambda < 9$; using a 1% level of significance

6 H_0: $\lambda = 3.5$; H_1: $\lambda < 3.5$; using a 5% level of significance

7 Every year a statistics teacher takes her class out to observe the traffic passing the school gates during a Tuesday lunch hour. Over the years she has established that the average number of lorries passing the gates in a lunch hour is 7.5. During the course of the last 12 months a new bypass has been built and the number of lorries passing the school gates in this year's experiment was 4. Test, at the 5% level, whether or not the mean number of lorries passing the gates during a Tuesday lunch hour has been reduced.

8 Over a long period, John has found that the bus taking him to school arrives late on average 9 times per month. In the month following the start of new summer schedules, John finds that his bus arrives late 13 times. Assuming that the number of times the bus is late has a Poisson distribution, test, at the 5% level of significance, whether the new schedules have in fact increased the number of times on which the bus is late. State clearly your null and alternative hypotheses.   [E]

SUMMARY OF KEY POINTS

1   A **population** is a collection of individual items.

2   A **sample** is a selection of individual members or items from a population.

3   A **finite population** is one in which each individual member can be given a number.

4   An **infinite population** is one in which it is impossible to number each member.

5   A **countably infinite population** is one which is infinite in size, but each member can be given an individual number.

6   A **sampling unit** is an individual member of a population.

7   A **sampling frame** is a list of sampling units used in practice to represent a population. In some instances the two will be identical, in others the sampling frame will represent the population as accurately as possible.

8   In practice a **sample** is a collection of sampling units drawn from a sampling frame.

9   A **hypothesis test** is a mathematical procedure to examine a value of a population parameter proposed by the null hypothesis H_0 compared with an alternative hypothesis H_1.

10 The **critical region** is the range of values of a test statistic T that would lead you to reject H_0.

Review exercise 2

1 By using a normal approximation for $X \sim B(80, 0.25)$ find:
   (a) $P(X > 18)$ (b) $P(X < 25)$
   (c) $P(X \geqslant 10)$ (d) $P(14 < X \leqslant 18)$

2 A horticulturist knows from experience that when taking leaf
   cuttings from bay trees only 15 in every 100 successfully take
   root.
   (a) In a batch of 10 randomly selected cuttings, find the
   probability that
    (i) none of the cuttings take root
   (ii) fewer than 3 of the cuttings take root.
   (b) Let n be the smallest number of cuttings which need to be
   examined before there is at least a 95% chance that one or
   more of them will have taken root.
    (i) Show that n satisfies $(0.85)^n \leqslant 0.05$
   (ii) Given that $(0.85)^{17} = 0.0631$, find the value of n.
   (c) Using a suitable approximation, estimate the probability
   that fewer than 6 in a batch of 50 cuttings take root.

3 State the conditions which are necessary for the use of a
   binomial distribution. Give an example of the use of a normal
   approximation to a binomial distribution, giving the parameters
   of the two distributions and stating any conditions which have
   to be satisfied in order that the approximation may be used.
   In a large restaurant one in four customers asks for iced water
   with a meal. Use normal distribution approximations to
   calculate:
   (a) the probability, to 4 decimal places, that of the first 100
   customers, fewer than 20 will ask for iced water with their meal
   (b) the smallest value of n such that there is a probability of
   at least 0.98 that fewer than n of 1000 customers will ask for
   iced water.   [E]

4 If a coin is tossed 1600 times the most likely result is 800 heads. Using a normal approximation estimate how likely this is.

5 The number of errors per page made by a typesetter for a publisher has a Poisson distribution with mean 4.

Find, to 3 decimal places, the probability that

(a) on any page there are fewer than 4 errors,

(b) in a 2-page document there are more than 10 errors,

(c) on 2 consecutive pages, there are exactly 2 errors on each page.

A new typesetter is employed and the number of errors made by the typesetter in setting a page is counted.

(d) State appropriate null and alternative hypotheses to test that the new typesetter is at least as reliable as the other typesetter.

(e) Derive a critical region, of approximate size 0.05, to test the null hypothesis.

State the exact size of your critical region.

(f) A page of the work done by the new typesetter is selected at random and is found to contain 6 errors.

What conclusion can you draw from this value? [E]

> The **size of a critical region** is the probability of rejecting H_0 when H_0 is true.

6 Explain briefly the circumstances under which a normal distribution may be used as an approximation to a binomial distribution. Give an example of the use of this approximation.

A large mixture of marrow seeds consists of two strains A and B in the ratio 4:1. Seeds are chosen at random from the mixture and planted in rows with 10 seeds in each row. Assuming that all the seeds germinate, find the mean and the variance of the number per row of plants of strain B.

Find an approximate value for the probability that in a total of 50 rows there will be more than 110 plants of strain B. [E]

7 The machines in a factory produce an average of nine defective items each during a normal working day. As part of the factory management's search for greater efficiency they discover a new type of machine, which, it is claimed, will produce fewer defective items. They are offered a one-day trial on one of these machines to test whether the average number of defective items produced is lower. They also assume a

Poisson distribution for the number of defective items produced by a single machine during a normal working day.

(a) State appropriate null and alternative hypotheses.

(b) Derive a critical region of size between 0.04 and 0.06 where the size of the critical region is defined as the probability that the alternative hypothesis is accepted given that the null hypothesis is true. State the exact size of the critical region.

(c) If six faulty items are produced by the new machine in the one-day trial, what conclusion should the factory management draw?   [E]

8 The continuous random variable Y has the rectangular distribution

$$f(y) = \begin{cases} \frac{1}{3}, & \frac{-3}{2} \leqslant y \leqslant \frac{3}{2}, \\ 0, & \text{otherwise.} \end{cases}$$

Find the mean and variance of Y.

9 State the condition under which a normal distribution may be used as an approximation to the Poisson distribution. Write down the mean and the variance of the normal approximation to the Poisson distribution with mean X. Tomatoes from a particular nursery are packed in boxes and sent to a market. Assuming that the number of bad tomatoes in a box has Poisson distribution with mean 0.44, find, to 3 significant figures, the probability of there being

if $p = 1.44$

p all good $\simeq 0.56$

(a) fewer than 2,

(b) more than 2 bad tomatoes in a box when it is opened. Use a normal approximation to find, to 3 decimal places, the probability that in 50 randomly chosen boxes there will be fewer than 20 bad tomatoes in total.   [E]

10 A sample of 4000 people are to be given a certain drug during a trial. It is known that there is a probability of 0.005 that any person has an adverse reaction to the drug. Use a suitable approximation to find the probability that less than 10 have an adverse reaction.

11 The weight of a randomly chosen plastic washer is normally distributed with mean 5 g.

(a) Calculate the standard deviation in grams given that the probability that a randomly chosen washer weighs less than 3 g is 0.123.

(b) Show that the probability that a randomly chosen washer weighs more than 9 g is 0.0102.

(c) Five washers are chosen at random. Calculate the probability that at least 2 weigh less than 3 g.

(d) Using a suitable approximation find the probability that out of 100 randomly chosen washers at least 3 weigh more than 9 g.

12 Five children chosen at random are asked to sample Energise Peanut Butter and Active Peanut Butter. Three of the children prefer the sample of Energise Peanut Butter. Does this show significant evidence that children in general prefer Energise Peanut Butter to Active Peanut Butter? Give reasons for your answer.

13 A large superstore sells an average of 6 top-of-the range dishwashers every day. After a price rise they sell 10 dishwashers over the next 5 days. Does this justify at the 5% significance level the statement 'the price rise has caused a significant drop in sales'?

14 State the conditions under which a Poisson distribution with parameter μ can be approximated by a normal distribution. State the mean and variance of the approximate distribution. The average number of lorries pulling into a motorway service station is 3 every 5 minutes.

(a) Explain why a Poisson distribution is suitable to model the number of lorries pulling into the service station per minute.

(b) Find, to 3 decimal places, the probability that in 10 minutes more than 7 lorries will pull into that service station.

(c) Estimate, giving your answer to 2 significant figures, the probability that more than 45 lorries will pull in during any one hour.

(d) When road works are started at the approach to the service station, the manager notices that during the next 4 hours only 100 lorries pull in. Assuming a Poisson model is still appropriate, perform a significance test at the 5% level to decide whether or not the average number of lorries pulling into the service station per hour has been reduced.

(e) Comment on the suitability of a Poisson model in (d). [E]

15 State whether the following variables are discrete or continuous giving reasons for your answers:

(a) daily rainfall

(b) growth rate of trees

(c) the cost of meals

(d) air temperature

16 Give two reasons why a factory inspector might choose to test a sample of components rather than the whole population.

17 For a sample survey of the lengths of leaves on a beech-tree suggest:

(a) a suitable sampling unit

(b) a suitable sampling frame.

18 At a children's party each child was blindfolded and asked to pin a tail on a cardboard donkey. The distance, in cm, of the pin from the correct position was measured and the results are recorded below

17, 15, 5, 9, 13, 42, 8, 24, 34, 38, 29, 6   240

(a) Find the mean and the standard deviation for this set of numbers.

$\mu = 20$

$\sigma = 12.5$ var $= 155.83$

A statistics student, who was helping at this party, attempts to model the distance, in cm, a child places the pin from the correct position using the continuous uniform distribution over the interval [0, 50].

$M = 25$

(b) Use the formulae on page 81 to find the mean and the standard deviation of this distribution. $\sigma - 14.43$

(c) Comment on the suitability of this distribution as a model in the present situation.   *not great*

The student attempts to refine the model and considers two distributions with probability density functions f(x) and g(x) illustrated below.

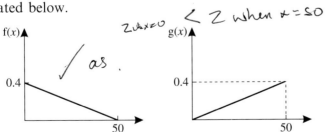

$2\nu \hbar x = 0$ < 2 when $x = 50$

$\sqrt{}$ as.

(d) Explain, giving a reason, which of these two probability density functions the student should choose.   [E]

19 Pak-a-Bik manufactures biscuits which are packed at random in boxes, each box containing 20 biscuits. The company produces 45% chocolate biscuits, the remainder being plain biscuits. 5% of all the biscuits made are wrapped in foil. A box is selected at random from the production line.

(a) Calculate the probability that this box contains more chocolate biscuits than plain biscuits.

The company quality assurance manager takes a random sample of 10 boxes of biscuits.

(b) Calculate the probability that exactly 4 of them contain more chocolate biscuits than plain ones.

For a special order, Pak-a-Bik produces a box containing 120 biscuits.

(c) Using suitable approximations calculate the probability that this box contains:

 (i) exactly 12 biscuits wrapped in foil

 (ii) at least 50 but not more than 60 chocolate biscuits.　　　[E]

20 By using a normal approximation for $X \sim$ Po (36) find:

(a) P(X = 36)　　　　(b) P(X ⩾ 30)

(c) P(X < 40)　　　　(d) P(32 < X ⩽ 39)

21 A study was done of the amount of pocket money received by English school children by taking 10 children from each class in a particular school.

State: (a) the sampling unit, (b) the sampling frame, (c) the population.

If the figures taken are used to represent the whole of England would the sample be unbiased?

22 A cricket team has 11 members. On every occasion they play the probability of any one of these regular players being unable to play is 0.15, independently of the other players.

(a) Calculate the probability that

 (i) exactly one member is unavailable to play,

 (ii) more than two members are unavailable to play.

(b) assuming that the probability of more than 3 players being unavailable is 0.06, what, in a 50 match season, would be the expected value of the number of matches for which more than 3 players are unavailable?

(c) Using a suitable approximation, find the probability that in a season more than 3 players will be unavailable in exactly 2 matches.

23 A trainer hypothesises that weight training affects running speeds. Assume that the trainer sets up a study to investigate the problem employing two different levels of weight training. Formulate H_0 and H_1.

24 Identify H_0 and H_1 in the following:
(a) The population mean intelligence is 100.
(b) The proportion of Liberals in X town is not equal to 0.6.
(c) The population mean intelligence is not equal to 100.
(d) The proportion of Liberals in X town is equal to 0.6.

25 A managing director wishes to test the hypothesis that there are not equal numbers of male and female executives in his group of companies. Which of the following would be an appropriate null hypothesis?
(a) There are more male than female executives.
(b) The number of males and female executives is equal.
(c) There are fewer male than female executives.

26 A test is set up with a null hypothesis such that $H_0 : \mu_1 = \mu_2$. List three possible hypotheses for H_1. Explain what effect these would have on the testing process.

27 Under what circumstances would it be sensible to use:
(a) the Normal distribution as an approximation to the binomial distribution?
(b) the Normal distribution as an approximation to the Poisson distribution?
(c) the Poisson distribution as an approximation to the binomial distribution?

28 The probability of a geranium germinating successfully from a seed is 0.6. If 10 seeds are planted by a gardener what is the probability that 7 will germinate?
If a garden centre plants 100 of the same seeds, using a suitable approximation find the probability that less than 60 will germinate.

29 A questionnaire given to a class of students contained the
following questions:
(a) What is your name? (b) What is your weight?
(c) What is your height? (d) Are you male or female?
(e) How many brothers and sisters do you have?
Which answers would be *qualitative* and which *quantitative*?

30 Describe the roles of the null and alternative hypotheses in a
test of significance. Explain how to decide whether the use of
a one-tail or a two-tail test is appropriate.
During the 7 years from 1950 to 1956 inclusive, electric
traction was used on 2500 miles of railway line. During these
years, 35 child trespassers were fatally electrocuted.
In a succeeding year, 3 children were fatally electrocuted on
one 100 mile stretch of the line in separate incidents.
Assuming that the numbers of children fatally electrocuted
have Poisson distributions, investigate whether this stretch of
line requires additional protection.   [E]

31 For each of the following populations state if they are finite,
infinite, or countably infinite:
(a) the number of throws at darts before getting a double
(b) the number of students in your school or college
(c) the number of kangaroos in Australia
(d) the number of spins of a roulette-wheel before a given
number comes up.

32 The continuous random variable X has a probability
distribution function f(x) as shown below.

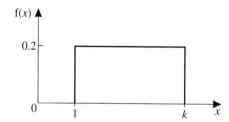

Find:
(a) value of k
(b) $(2.4 \leqslant X \leqslant 3)$
(c) $E(X)$
(d) $Var(X)$

33 The probability of Brand A lotion curing a particular skin complaint is 0.35. It is thought that a new lotion Brand B will improve the cure rate. Brand B lotion was tested on 20 people and 10 people were cured of the problem. Stating your null and alternative hypotheses show why the new cure rate of Brand B is not significant at the 5% level. How many of the 20 people tested would need to be cured before the results would be significant at the 5% level?

34 A pickling machine broke down on average 5 times per week. A modification was introduced and, in the week following its introduction, the machine only broke down twice. Does this provide significant evidence at the 5% level to support the theory that the modification has reduced breakdowns?

Examination style paper

S2

Answer all questions   **Time allowed $1\frac{1}{2}$ hours**

1. Explain briefly what you understand by
   (a) a statistical model   (b) a sampling unit
   (c) a sampling frame.

   (4 marks)

2. (a) Write down the conditions needed to be able to approximate the binomial distribution by the Poisson distribution.
   ✓ The random variable $X \sim B(400, 0.02)$. $n = large \quad p = small$
   (b) Use a Poisson approximation to estimate $P(X = 7)$.

        $mean \sim 8$ $p7 = e^{-8} \times \dfrac{8^7}{7!} = 0.1396$ **(6 marks)**

3. The continuous random variable Y is uniformly distributed over the interval $(3, 7)$.
   Find
   (a) $E(Y)$ 5 (b) $Var(Y)$ (c) $P(4.2 \leqslant Y \leqslant 5.9)$.

   (7 marks)

4. Balloons are packed at random and sold in packets containing 20 balloons.
   ✓ The company manufacturing the balloons produce 45% blue ones and the remainder are red ones.
   A packet is selected at random from the production line.
   (a) Write down two reasons to support the use of the binomial $independent$ $\wedge fixed$ distribution to model the number of blue balloons in a packet. $p \,fixed$
   (b) Calculate the probability that this packet contains $\sim (20, 0.45)$
   (i) exactly 7 blue balloons $p(7) = 0.45^7 \times 0.55^{13} \times \, 20C_7 = 0.1221$
   (ii) more blue balloons than red balloons. $p \, atleast \, 11 = 1 - p(less than or 10) = 1 - 0.7507 = 0.2493$
   A random sample of 10 packets of balloons is selected.
   (c) Find the probability that exactly four of them contain more blue than red balloons. $or \quad p = 0.2493 \quad n = 10$ $0.2493^4 \times 0.7507^6 \times 10C_4$

        $10 \, packets$ **(9 marks)** $= 0.1482$

5. State conditions under which the Poisson distribution is a suitable model to use in statistical work.

   Flaws in a certain brand of rope occur at random and at an average of 0.70 per 100 metres. Assuming a Poisson distribution for the number of flaws, find the probability that in a 400 metre long piece of rope

   $0.7 \times 4 = 2.8$

   (a) there will be at least one flaw, $P(\text{at least } 1) = 1 - P(0) = 1 - e^{-2.8} = 0.9392$
   (b) there will be at most 2 flaws. $P(0,1,2) = 0.0608$

   Find the probability that in a batch of 5 pieces of rope, each of length 400 metres, all 5 pieces will contain fewer than 3 flaws.

   (14 marks)

6. The random variable X has probability density function

   $$f(x) = \begin{cases} 1 - \frac{1}{4}x, & 1 \leqslant x \leqslant 3, \\ 0, & \text{otherwise.} \end{cases}$$

   (a) Sketch $f(x)$.
   (b) Find $E(X)$.
   (c) Show that $P(X > E(X)) = 0.462$ (3 d.p.)
   (d) Determine whether the median of X is greater or less than $E(X)$.

   (16 marks)

7. A manufacturer of coloured drawing pins decides to introduce a purple pin. The pins are sold in boxes of 20 and the purple ones make up 15% of the total production. A teacher buys a box of pins and discovers that it contains only one purple pin.

   (a) Stating your hypotheses clearly test, at the 5% level of significance, whether or not there is evidence that the percentage of purple pins in a box is less than 15.

   (b) State, giving a reason, the number of purple pins in a box that would be required to obtain a significant result to the test above.

   (c) State an assumption that has been made about the filling of the boxes.

   The teacher bought another four boxes of pins and the numbers of purple pins they contained were 3, 1, 2 and 1.

   (d) By combining the results of all 5 boxes, and using a suitable approximation, test at the 5% level of significance whether or not the combined results provide evidence that the percentage of purple pins is less than 15.

   (e) Comment briefly on your answer to these two tests.

   (19 marks)

Appendix

Table 1 Binomial cumulative distribution function

The tabulated value is $P(X \leqslant x)$, where X has a binomial distribution with index n and parameter p.

$p =$	0.05	0.10	0.15	0.20	0.25	0.30	0.35	0.40	0.45	0.50
$n = 5, x = 0$	0.7738	0.5905	0.4437	0.3277	0.2373	0.1681	0.1160	0.0778	0.0503	0.0312
1	0.9774	0.9185	0.8352	0.7373	0.6328	0.5282	0.4284	0.3370	0.2562	0.1875
2	0.9988	0.9914	0.9734	0.9421	0.8965	0.8369	0.7648	0.6826	0.5931	0.5000
3	1.0000	0.9995	0.9978	0.9933	0.9844	0.9692	0.9460	0.9130	0.8688	0.8125
4	1.0000	1.0000	0.9999	0.9997	0.9990	0.9976	0.9947	0.9898	0.9815	0.9688
$n = 10, x = 0$	0.5987	0.3487	0.1969	0.1074	0.0563	0.0282	0.0135	0.0060	0.0025	0.0010
1	0.9139	0.7361	0.5443	0.3758	0.2440	0.1493	0.0860	0.0464	0.0233	0.0107
2	0.9885	0.9298	0.8202	0.6778	0.5256	0.3828	0.2616	0.1673	0.0996	0.0547
3	0.9990	0.9872	0.9500	0.8791	0.7759	0.6496	0.5138	0.3823	0.2660	0.1719
4	0.9999	0.9984	0.9901	0.9672	0.9219	0.8497	0.7515	0.6331	0.5044	0.3770
5	1.0000	0.9999	0.9986	0.9936	0.9803	0.9527	0.9051	0.8338	0.7384	0.6230
6	1.0000	1.0000	0.9999	0.9991	0.9965	0.9894	0.9740	0.9452	0.8980	0.8281
7	1.0000	1.0000	1.0000	0.9999	0.9996	0.9984	0.9952	0.9877	0.9726	0.9453
8	1.0000	1.0000	1.0000	1.0000	1.0000	0.9999	0.9995	0.9983	0.9955	0.9893
9	1.0000	1.0000	1.0000	1.0000	1.0000	1.0000	1.0000	0.9999	0.9997	0.9990
$n = 20, x = 0$	0.3585	0.1216	0.0388	0.0115	0.0032	0.0008	0.0002	0.0000	0.0000	0.0000
1	0.7358	0.3917	0.1756	0.0692	0.0243	0.0076	0.0021	0.0005	0.0001	0.0000
2	0.9245	0.6769	0.4049	0.2061	0.0913	0.0355	0.0121	0.0036	0.0009	0.0002
3	0.9841	0.8670	0.6477	0.4114	0.2252	0.1071	0.0444	0.0160	0.0049	0.0013
4	0.9974	0.9568	0.8298	0.6296	0.4148	0.2375	0.1182	0.0510	0.0189	0.0059
5	0.9997	0.9887	0.9327	0.8042	0.6172	0.4164	0.2454	0.1256	0.0553	0.0207
6	1.0000	0.9976	0.9781	0.9133	0.7858	0.6080	0.4166	0.2500	0.1299	0.0577
7	1.0000	0.9996	0.9941	0.9679	0.8982	0.7723	0.6010	0.4159	0.2520	0.1316
8	1.0000	0.9999	0.9987	0.9900	0.9591	0.8867	0.7624	0.5956	0.4143	0.2517
9	1.0000	1.0000	0.9998	0.9974	0.9861	0.9520	0.8782	0.7553	0.5914	0.4119
10	1.0000	1.0000	1.0000	0.9994	0.9961	0.9829	0.9468	0.8725	0.7507	0.5881
11	1.0000	1.0000	1.0000	0.9999	0.9991	0.9949	0.9804	0.9435	0.8692	0.7483
12	1.0000	1.0000	1.0000	1.0000	0.9998	0.9987	0.9940	0.9790	0.9420	0.8684
13	1.0000	1.0000	1.0000	1.0000	1.0000	0.9997	0.9985	0.9935	0.9786	0.9423
14	1.0000	1.0000	1.0000	1.0000	1.0000	1.0000	0.9997	0.9984	0.9936	0.9793
15	1.0000	1.0000	1.0000	1.0000	1.0000	1.0000	1.0000	0.9997	0.9985	0.9941
16	1.0000	1.0000	1.0000	1.0000	1.0000	1.0000	1.0000	1.0000	0.9997	0.9987
17	1.0000	1.0000	1.0000	1.0000	1.0000	1.0000	1.0000	1.0000	1.0000	0.9998
18	1.0000	1.0000	1.0000	1.0000	1.0000	1.0000	1.0000	1.0000	1.0000	1.0000

Table 2 Poisson cumulative distribution function

The tabulated value is $P(X \leqslant x)$, where X has a Poisson distribution with parameter λ.

$\lambda =$	0.5	1.0	1.5	2.0	2.5	3.0	3.5	4.0	4.5	5.0
$x = 0$	0.6065	0.3679	0.2231	0.1353	0.0821	0.0498	0.0302	0.0183	0.0111	0.0067
1	0.9098	0.7358	0.5578	0.4060	0.2873	0.1991	0.1359	0.0916	0.0611	0.0404
2	0.9856	0.9197	0.8088	0.6767	0.5438	0.4232	0.3208	0.2381	0.1736	0.1247
3	0.9982	0.9810	0.9344	0.8571	0.7576	0.6472	0.5366	0.4335	0.3423	0.2650
4	0.9998	0.9963	0.9814	0.9473	0.8912	0.8153	0.7254	0.6288	0.5321	0.4405
5	1.0000	0.9994	0.9955	0.9834	0.9580	0.9161	0.8576	0.7851	0.7029	0.6160
6	1.0000	0.9999	0.9991	0.9955	0.9858	0.9665	0.9347	0.8893	0.8311	0.7622
7	1.0000	1.0000	0.9998	0.9989	0.9958	0.9881	0.9733	0.9489	0.9134	0.8666
8	1.0000	1.0000	1.0000	0.9998	0.9989	0.9962	0.9901	0.9786	0.9597	0.9319
9	1.0000	1.0000	1.0000	1.0000	0.9997	0.9989	0.9967	0.9919	0.9829	0.9682
10	1.0000	1.0000	1.0000	1.0000	0.9999	0.9997	0.9990	0.9972	0.9933	0.9863
11	1.0000	1.0000	1.0000	1.0000	1.0000	0.9999	0.9997	0.9991	0.9976	0.9945
12	1.0000	1.0000	1.0000	1.0000	1.0000	1.0000	0.9999	0.9997	0.9992	0.9980
13	1.0000	1.0000	1.0000	1.0000	1.0000	1.0000	1.0000	0.9999	0.9997	0.9993
14	1.0000	1.0000	1.0000	1.0000	1.0000	1.0000	1.0000	1.0000	0.9999	0.9998
15	1.0000	1.0000	1.0000	1.0000	1.0000	1.0000	1.0000	1.0000	1.0000	0.9999
16	1.0000	1.0000	1.0000	1.0000	1.0000	1.0000	1.0000	1.0000	1.0000	1.0000
17	1.0000	1.0000	1.0000	1.0000	1.0000	1.0000	1.0000	1.0000	1.0000	1.0000
18	1.0000	1.0000	1.0000	1.0000	1.0000	1.0000	1.0000	1.0000	1.0000	1.0000
19	1.0000	1.0000	1.0000	1.0000	1.0000	1.0000	1.0000	1.0000	1.0000	1.0000

$\lambda =$	5.5	6.0	6.5	7.0	7.5	8.0	8.5	9.0	9.5	10.0
$x = 0$	0.0041	0.0025	0.0015	0.0009	0.0006	0.0003	0.0002	0.0001	0.0001	0.0000
1	0.0266	0.0174	0.0113	0.0073	0.0047	0.0030	0.0019	0.0012	0.0008	0.0005
2	0.0884	0.0620	0.0430	0.0296	0.0203	0.0138	0.0093	0.0062	0.0042	0.0028
3	0.2017	0.1512	0.1118	0.0818	0.0591	0.0424	0.0301	0.0212	0.0149	0.0103
4	0.3575	0.2851	0.2237	0.1730	0.1321	0.0996	0.0744	0.0550	0.0403	0.0293
5	0.5289	0.4457	0.3690	0.3007	0.2414	0.1912	0.1496	0.1157	0.0885	0.0671
6	0.6860	0.6063	0.5265	0.4497	0.3782	0.3134	0.2562	0.2068	0.1649	0.1301
7	0.8095	0.7440	0.6728	0.5987	0.5246	0.4530	0.3856	0.3239	0.2687	0.2202
8	0.8944	0.8472	0.7916	0.7291	0.6620	0.5925	0.5231	0.4557	0.3918	0.3328
9	0.9462	0.9161	0.8774	0.8305	0.7764	0.7166	0.6530	0.5874	0.5218	0.4579
10	0.9747	0.9574	0.9332	0.9015	0.8622	0.8159	0.7634	0.7060	0.6453	0.5830
11	0.9890	0.9799	0.9661	0.9467	0.9208	0.8881	0.8487	0.8030	0.7520	0.6968
12	0.9955	0.9912	0.9840	0.9730	0.9573	0.9362	0.9091	0.8758	0.8364	0.7916
13	0.9983	0.9964	0.9929	0.9872	0.9784	0.9658	0.9486	0.9261	0.8981	0.8645
14	0.9994	0.9986	0.9970	0.9943	0.9897	0.9827	0.9726	0.9585	0.9400	0.9165
15	0.9998	0.9995	0.9988	0.9976	0.9954	0.9918	0.9862	0.9780	0.9665	0.9513
16	0.9999	0.9998	0.9996	0.9990	0.9980	0.9963	0.9934	0.9889	0.9823	0.9730
17	1.0000	0.9999	0.9998	0.9996	0.9992	0.9984	0.9970	0.9947	0.9911	0.9857
18	1.0000	1.0000	0.9999	0.9999	0.9997	0.9993	0.9987	0.9976	0.9957	0.9928
19	1.0000	1.0000	1.0000	1.0000	0.9999	0.9997	0.9995	0.9989	0.9980	0.9965
20	1.0000	1.0000	1.0000	1.0000	1.0000	0.9999	0.9998	0.9996	0.9991	0.9984
21	1.0000	1.0000	1.0000	1.0000	1.0000	1.0000	0.9999	0.9998	0.9996	0.9993
22	1.0000	1.0000	1.0000	1.0000	1.0000	1.0000	1.0000	0.9999	0.9999	0.9997

Table 3 The normal distribution function

The function tabulated below is $\Phi(z)$, defined as

$$\Phi(z) = \frac{1}{\sqrt{2\pi}} \int_{-\infty}^{z} e^{-\frac{1}{2}t^2} dt.$$

z	$\Phi(z)$	z	$\Phi(z)$	z	$\Phi(z)$	z	$\Phi(z)$	z	$\Phi(z)$
0.00	0.5000	0.50	0.6915	1.00	0.8413	1.50	0.9332	2.00	0.9772
0.01	0.5040	0.51	0.6950	1.01	0.8438	1.51	0.9345	2.02	0.9783
0.02	0.5080	0.52	0.6985	1.02	0.8461	1.52	0.9357	2.04	0.9793
0.03	0.5120	0.53	0.7019	1.03	0.8485	1.53	0.9370	2.06	0.9803
0.04	0.5160	0.54	0.7054	1.04	0.8508	1.54	0.9382	2.08	0.9812
0.05	0.5199	0.55	0.7088	1.05	0.8531	1.55	0.9394	2.10	0.9821
0.06	0.5239	0.56	0.7123	1.06	0.8554	1.56	0.9406	2.12	0.9830
0.07	0.5279	0.57	0.7157	1.07	0.8577	1.57	0.9418	2.14	0.9838
0.08	0.5319	0.58	0.7190	1.08	0.8599	1.58	0.9429	2.16	0.9846
0.09	0.5359	0.59	0.7224	1.09	0.8621	1.59	0.9441	2.18	0.9854
0.10	0.5398	0.60	0.7257	1.10	0.8643	1.60	0.9452	2.20	0.9861
0.11	0.5438	0.61	0.7291	1.11	0.8665	1.61	0.9463	2.22	0.9868
0.12	0.5478	0.62	0.7324	1.12	0.8686	1.62	0.9474	2.24	0.9875
0.13	0.5517	0.63	0.7357	1.13	0.8708	1.63	0.9484	2.26	0.9881
0.14	0.5557	0.64	0.7389	1.14	0.8729	1.64	0.9495	2.28	0.9887
0.15	0.5596	0.65	0.7422	1.15	0.8749	1.65	0.9505	2.30	0.9893
0.16	0.5636	0.66	0.7454	1.16	0.8770	1.66	0.9515	2.32	0.9898
0.17	0.5675	0.67	0.7486	1.17	0.8790	1.67	0.9525	2.34	0.9904
0.18	0.5714	0.68	0.7517	1.18	0.8810	1.68	0.9535	2.36	0.9909
0.19	0.5753	0.69	0.7549	1.19	0.8830	1.69	0.9545	2.38	0.9913
0.20	0.5793	0.70	0.7580	1.20	0.8849	1.70	0.9554	2.40	0.9918
0.21	0.5832	0.71	0.7611	1.21	0.8869	1.71	0.9564	2.42	0.9922
0.22	0.5871	0.72	0.7642	1.22	0.8888	1.72	0.9573	2.44	0.9927
0.23	0.5910	0.73	0.7673	1.23	0.8907	1.73	0.9582	2.46	0.9931
0.24	0.5948	0.74	0.7704	1.24	0.8925	1.74	0.9591	2.48	0.9934
0.25	0.5987	0.75	0.7734	1.25	0.8944	1.75	0.9599	2.50	0.9938
0.26	0.6026	0.76	0.7764	1.26	0.8962	1.76	0.9608	2.55	0.9946
0.27	0.6064	0.77	0.7794	1.27	0.8980	1.77	0.9616	2.60	0.9953
0.28	0.6103	0.78	0.7823	1.28	0.8997	1.78	0.9625	2.65	0.9960
0.29	0.6141	0.79	0.7852	1.29	0.9015	1.79	0.9633	2.70	0.9965
0.30	0.6179	0.80	0.7881	1.30	0.9032	1.80	0.9641	2.75	0.9970
0.31	0.6217	0.81	0.7910	1.31	0.9049	1.81	0.9649	2.80	0.9974
0.32	0.6255	0.82	0.7939	1.32	0.9066	1.82	0.9656	2.85	0.9978
0.33	0.6293	0.83	0.7967	1.33	0.9082	1.83	0.9664	2.90	0.9981
0.34	0.6331	0.84	0.7995	1.34	0.9099	1.84	0.9671	2.95	0.9984
0.35	0.6368	0.85	0.8023	1.35	0.9115	1.85	0.9678	3.00	0.9987
0.36	0.6406	0.86	0.8051	1.36	0.9131	1.86	0.9686	3.05	0.9989
0.37	0.6443	0.87	0.8078	1.37	0.9147	1.87	0.9693	3.10	0.9990
0.38	0.6480	0.88	0.8106	1.38	0.9162	1.88	0.9699	3.15	0.9992
0.39	0.6517	0.89	0.8133	1.39	0.9177	1.89	0.9706	3.20	0.9993
0.40	0.6554	0.90	0.8159	1.40	0.9192	1.90	0.9713	3.25	0.9994
0.41	0.6591	0.91	0.8186	1.41	0.9207	1.91	0.9719	3.30	0.9995
0.42	0.6628	0.92	0.8212	1.42	0.9222	1.92	0.9726	3.35	0.9996
0.43	0.6664	0.93	0.8238	1.43	0.9236	1.93	0.9732	3.40	0.9997
0.44	0.6700	0.94	0.8264	1.44	0.9251	1.94	0.9738	3.50	0.9998
0.45	0.6736	0.95	0.8289	1.45	0.9265	1.95	0.9744	3.60	0.9998
0.46	0.6772	0.96	0.8315	1.46	0.9279	1.96	0.9750	3.70	0.9999
0.47	0.6808	0.97	0.8340	1.47	0.9292	1.97	0.9756	3.80	0.9999
0.48	0.6844	0.98	0.8365	1.48	0.9306	1.98	0.9761	3.90	1.0000
0.49	0.6879	0.99	0.8389	1.49	0.9319	1.99	0.9767	4.00	1.0000
0.50	0.6915	1.00	0.8413	1.50	0.9332	2.00	0.9772		

Table 4 Percentage points of the normal distribution

The values z in the table are those which a random variable $Z \sim N(0, 1)$ exceeds with probability p; that is, $P(Z > z) = 1 - \Phi(z) = p$.

p	z	p	z
0.5000	0.0000	0.0500	1.6449
0.4000	0.2533	0.0250	1.9600
0.3000	0.5244	0.0100	2.3263
0.2000	0.8416	0.0050	2.5758
0.1500	1.0364	0.0010	3.0902
0.1000	1.2816	0.0005	3.2905

Answers

Exercise 1A

1 (a) 10   (b) 1287   (c) 35   (d) 15
   (e) 6435   (f) 924   (g) 19 448 (h) 9
2 (a) $\frac{21}{2584}$ (b) $\frac{25}{1938}$ (c) $\frac{63}{1292}$ (d) $\frac{9}{38}$
3 (a) $\frac{59\,049}{3\,200\,000}$ (b) $\frac{27}{1600}$ (c) $\frac{19\,683}{320\,000}$ (d) $\frac{81}{400}$

Exercise 1B

1 $p^4 + 4p^3q + 6p^2q^2 + 4pq^3 + q^4$
2 $p^6 + 6p^5q + 15p^4q^2 + 20p^3q^3 + 15p^2q^4 + 6pq^5 + q^6$
3 (a) $120p^3q^7$ (b) $210p^6q^4$ (c) $45p^8q^2$
4 (a) $495p^4q^8$ (b) $495p^8q^4$ (c) $66p^{10}q^2$
5 $A = 105, x = 2; B = 455, y = 3;$
   $C = 1365, z = 4$
6 $A = 286, x = 3; B = 715, y = 4;$
   $C = 1287, z = 5$
7 77 520
8 $A = 15\,504, x = 5$
9 (a) 0.0163   (b) 0.1366   (c) 0.0569
10 (a) $A = 56, x = 3;$ 0.0231
    (b) $B = 56, y = 5;$ 0.2076
    (c) $C = 28, z = 6;$ 0.0038

Exercise 1C

1 (a) 0.2731   (b) 0.4682   (c) 0.8049
2 (a) 0.1318   (b) 0.8306   (c) 0.0376
3 (a) 0.1766   (b) 0.1419   (c) 0.7583
4 (a) 0.2001   (b) 0.5981   (c) 0.2018
5 (a) 0.9740   (b) 0.2485   (c) 0.0689
   (d) 0.4814

6 (a) 0.4019   (b) 0.5981   (c) 0.9999
7 (a) 0.25   (b) $\frac{15}{16}$ (c) $\frac{3}{8}$
8 (a) 0.3585   (b) 0.1887   (c) 0.9841
9 (a) Bolts independent, $n = 20$, $p = 0.01$
   (b) Lights independent, $n = 6$, $p = 0.52$
   (c) Serves independent, prob. of ace constant,
   $n = 30$, $p = \frac{1}{8}$
10 (a) Yes; $B(14, 0.15)$ (b) No; n not fixed
    (c) Yes; $B(15, 0.12)$
11 (a) $\frac{16}{243}$ (b) 0.307
12 $\frac{16}{27}$
13 (a) 0.058   (b) 0.448
14 Method I: 0.987, Method II: 0.983
    ; Use Method I.

Exercise 1D

1 (a) $\mu = 3; \sigma^2 = 2.25$ (b) 0.6840
2 (a) $\mu = 3; \sigma^2 = 2$ (b) 0.5072
3 (a) $n = 60$ (b) $\sigma = 1.69$
4 7
5 $p = \frac{1}{2}$
6 0.086; 60; 90

Exercise 1E

1 (a) 0.2052   (b) 0.4562   (c) 0.9580
   (d) 0.4142
2 (a) 0.1125   (b) 0.0611   (c) 0.4679
   (d) 0.7700
3 (a) 0.2019   (b) 0.4751   (c) 0.7834
   (d) 0.3963
4 (a) 0.8088   (b) 0.0474   (c) 0.1438
   (d) 0.0460
5 (a) 6   (b) 9   (c) 5   (d) 5

6 (a) 5 (b) 2 (c) $\geqslant 7$ (d) $\geqslant 9$

7 (a) $\geqslant 9$ (b) $\geqslant 10$ (c) $\leqslant 2$ (d) $\geqslant 12$

8 (a) 0.2865 (b) 0.3554

9 (a) 0.1730 (b) 0.0302

10 (a) 0.0235 (b) 0.0293

    (c) defects occur randomly

11 (a) Yes – if they occur randomly

    (b) Yes – pigs randomly dispersed

    (c) No – pigs clustered

    (d) No – salt needs to diffuse

    (e) Yes but possible clustering.

12 (a) 0.067 (b) 0.083

13 (a) 0.908 (b) 9

14 (a) 0.2707 (b) 5.3

15 (a) 0.251 (b) 0.587

16 (a) (i) 0.223 (ii) 0.442 (b) 0.099

17 (a) 0.303 (b) 0.028

18 (a) 0.504 (b) 0.088

Exercise 1F

1 (a) 0.0174 (b) 0.1339

2 (a) 0.0235 (b) 0.8883

3 (a) 0.0337 (b) 0.0843 (c) 0.8753

4 (a) 0.0183 (b) 0.0733 (c) 0.2381

5 (a) 4.5×10^{-5} (b) 0.0671

6 0.0099; 0.323

7 0.016; (a) 0.908 (b) 0.004; 0.0003

8 np, np; 0.963; 0.3; 0.857

Exercise 1G

1 (a) Events occur singly, at random, independently, in continuous space or time.

    (b) 0.950 (d) 0.70

2 (a) 0.879 (b) 0.773 (c) 0.776 (d) $m = 7$

3 (a) 0.618 (b) 0.224 (c) 0.125 (d) 0.08

4 (a) 0.221 (b) 0.998 (d) 0.925

5 (a) Poisson $\lambda = 0.25$ (b) 0.221

6 (a) Poisson; currants must be evenly distributed

    (b) $\lambda = 7.5$ (d) 0.984

7 0.00098; 0.0547

Exercise 2A

1 (a) continuous (b) discrete

    (c) discrete (d) continuous

2 (a) no, area > 1 (b) no, f(1) < 0

    (c) yes

3 (a) $k = \frac{2}{3}$ (b) $k = \frac{1}{2}$

4 (a) $a = \frac{3}{8}$ (b) $a = \frac{3}{28}$

5 (a) $a = 1$ (b) $a = \frac{2}{3}$ (c) $a = \frac{1}{\sqrt{2}}$

6 (a) no, f(−1) < 0 (b) no, area > 1

    (c) yes

7 (a) no, f(x) < 0 (b) no, area ≠ 1

    (c) no, area ≠ 1

8 (a) no, f(x) < 0 (b) yes

    (c) no, $k = \frac{5}{2} \Rightarrow$ f(2) < 0

9 (a) $f(x) = \begin{cases} 2 - 2x & 0 \leqslant x \leqslant 1 \\ 0 & \text{otherwise} \end{cases}$

    (b) $f(x) = \begin{cases} \frac{3}{2}x + 1 & 0 \leqslant x \leqslant \frac{2}{3} \\ 0 & \text{otherwise} \end{cases}$

    (c) $f(x) = \begin{cases} \frac{2}{5} & 0 \leqslant x < 2 \\ \frac{2}{5}(3 - x) & 2 \leqslant x \leqslant 3 \\ 0 & \text{otherwise} \end{cases}$

10 (a) (b)

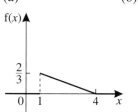
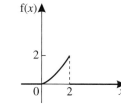

    (c) (d)

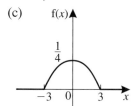
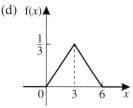

Exercise 2B

1 (a) $\frac{3}{4}$ (b) $\frac{3}{4}$ (c) $\frac{1}{2}$

2 (a) $\frac{5}{12}$ (b) $f(x) = \begin{cases} \frac{2}{3}x & 1 \leqslant x \leqslant 2 \\ 0 & \text{otherwise} \end{cases}$

3 (a) $F(x) = \begin{cases} 0 & x < 0 \\ \dfrac{x^3}{8} & 0 \leqslant x < 2 \\ 1 & x \geqslant 2 \end{cases}$

    (b) $\frac{1}{8}$

4 (a) $f(x) = \begin{cases} \dfrac{2x}{5} & 2 \leqslant x < 3 \\ 0 & \text{otherwise} \end{cases}$

(b) $f(x) = \begin{cases} \frac{1}{9}(6x^2 - 5) & 1 \leqslant x \leqslant 2 \\ 0 & \text{otherwise} \end{cases}$

5 (a) $a = 2$ (b) $a = -\frac{1}{2}$

6 (a) $a = 2$, $b = \frac{1}{56}$

(b) $f(x) = \begin{cases} \frac{1}{56}(6x^2 + 2) & 1 \leqslant x \leqslant 3 \\ 0 & \text{otherwise} \end{cases}$

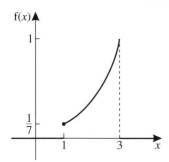

7 (a) $f(x) = \begin{cases} \frac{1}{2}(3x^2 - 4x + 1) & 1 \leqslant x \leqslant 2 \\ 0 & \text{otherwise} \end{cases}$

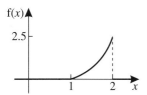

(b) 0.1875

8 (a) no; $F'(1) < 0$ (b) no; $F'(2) < 0$

(c) yes: $f(x) = \begin{cases} \frac{15}{2}x^2(1 - x^2) & 0 \leqslant x \leqslant 1 \\ 0 & \text{otherwise} \end{cases}$

(d) no; $F'(4) < 0$

9 (a) $F(x) = \begin{cases} 0 & x < -3 \\ \frac{1}{36}\left(18 + 9x - \dfrac{x^3}{3}\right) & -3 \leqslant x \leqslant 3 \\ 1 & x > 3 \end{cases}$

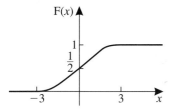

(b) $F(x) = \begin{cases} 0 & x < 0 \\ \dfrac{x^2}{18} & 0 \leqslant x < 3 \\ \frac{1}{18}(-18 + 12x - x^2) & 3 \leqslant x < 6 \\ 1 & x \geqslant 6 \end{cases}$

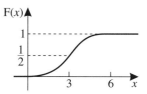

10 (a) $F_X(x) = \begin{cases} 0 & x < 0 \\ \dfrac{x^2}{4} & 0 \leqslant x \leqslant 2 \\ 1 & x > 2 \end{cases}$

(d) $f(x) = \begin{cases} \frac{1}{4} & 0 \leqslant y \leqslant 0 \\ 0 & \text{otherwise} \end{cases}$

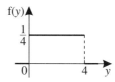

Exercise 2C

1 (a) 2 (b) $\frac{1}{3}$ (d) $\frac{4}{9}$

2 (a) $\frac{10}{9}$ (b) $\frac{26}{81}$ (c) $\frac{5}{12}$ (d) $\frac{128}{243}$

3 (a) $\frac{5}{16}$ (b) $\frac{3}{5}$

4 (a)   (b) 0 (d) 0.54

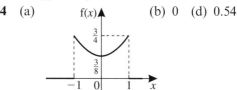

5 (a) $\frac{1}{4}$ (c) $\frac{1}{16}$

6 (b) $F(t) = \begin{cases} 0 & t < 0 \\ \frac{1}{1000}t^3 & 0 \leqslant t \leqslant 10 \\ 1 & t > 10 \end{cases}$ (c) 0.386

(d)   (e)

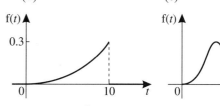

7 (a) 2 (b) $\frac{3}{4}$

8 (b) £102.19 (c) £10.22 (d) £13.61

9 (a) $\frac{1}{2500}$ (b) $\frac{16}{3}$ (c) 2.21 (d) 0.9216; 0.0064

10 (a) 0 (b) $\frac{\pi^2}{12}$

Exercise 2D

1 (b) 0

(c)
$$F(x) = \begin{cases} 0 & x < 0 \\ x - \frac{1}{4}x^2 & 0 \leqslant x \leqslant 2 \\ 1 & x > 2 \end{cases}$$

(d) $2 - \sqrt{2}$

2 (b) 0

(c)
$$F(y) = \begin{cases} 0 & y < 0 \\ \frac{1}{2}y - \frac{y^2}{18} & 0 \leqslant y \leqslant 3 \\ 1 & y > 3 \end{cases}$$

(d) $\left(\dfrac{9 - 3\sqrt{5}}{2} \right)$

3 (b) 2

(c)
$$F(x) = \begin{cases} 0 & x < 0 \\ \frac{x^4}{16} & 0 \leqslant x \leqslant 2 \\ 1 & x > 2 \end{cases}$$

(d) 1.68

4 (b) Bimodal at -1 and 1 (c) 0

(d)
$$F(x) = \begin{cases} 0 & x < -1 \\ \frac{x^3}{8} + \frac{3}{8}x + \frac{1}{2} & -1 \leqslant x \leqslant 1 \\ 1 & x > 1 \end{cases}$$

5 (b) mode = median = 0

(c)
$$F(x) = \begin{cases} 0 & x < -2 \\ \frac{1}{2} + \frac{3x}{8} - \frac{x^3}{32} & -2 \leqslant x \leqslant 2 \\ 1 & x > 2 \end{cases}$$

6 (b) 1.5

(c)
$$F(x) = \begin{cases} 0 & x < 0 \\ \frac{x^2}{20}(9 - 2x) & 0 \leqslant x \leqslant 2 \\ 1 & x > 2 \end{cases}$$

7 (a)
$$f(x) = \begin{cases} 12x^2(1-x) & 0 \leqslant x \leqslant 1 \\ 0 & \text{otherwise} \end{cases}$$

(b) $\frac{2}{3}$ (c) 0.2853

8 (a)
$$f(x) = \begin{cases} \dfrac{x}{4} & 1 \leqslant x \leqslant 3 \\ 0 & \text{otherwise} \end{cases}$$

(b) 3 (c) $\sqrt{5}$ (d) $\sqrt{3}, \sqrt{7}$

9 Possible answers are:

(a) $\frac{4}{9}x + \frac{1}{27}(1-x)^3 - \frac{1}{27}$ (b) $\frac{4}{9} - \frac{1}{9}(1-x)^2$

10 (a)
$$F(w) = \begin{cases} 0 & w < 0 \\ \dfrac{w^4}{5^5}(25 - 4w) & 0 \leqslant w \leqslant 5 \\ 1 & w > 5 \end{cases}$$

(b) 0.650

11
$$F(x) = \begin{cases} 0 & x < 0 \\ \dfrac{x}{4} & 0 \leqslant x \leqslant 1 \\ \dfrac{1}{5} + \dfrac{x^4}{20} & 1 \leqslant x \leqslant 2 \\ 1 & x > 2 \end{cases}$$

median 1.565

I.Q.R. 0.821

Review exercise 1

1 Discrete: a, d, e

Continuous: b, c, f, g

2 binomial: a, d; Poisson: b, c, e, f

3 For a Poisson they will be equal. Events occur randomly; events occur singly; events occur independently.

4 (a) 0.05   (b) 0.05

5 (a)
$$f(x) = \begin{cases} 2x & 0 \leqslant x \leqslant 1 \\ 0 & \text{otherwise} \end{cases}$$

(b)
$$F(x) = \begin{cases} 0 & x \leqslant 0 \\ x^2 & 0 < x \leqslant 1 \\ 1 & x > 1 \end{cases}$$

(c) $\frac{2}{3}, \frac{1}{\sqrt{2}} = 0.707$

(d) 0.25

6 0.751; 0.537

7 (a) $k = \frac{2}{3}$ (b) $1\frac{2}{9}, 1\frac{13}{18}$ (c) 1.25

8 Po(1.49) (a) 0.226 (b) 0.812

9 (a) 10 (b) 0.00674

10 (a) (i) 0.679 (ii) 0.995 (b) 0.473

11 (b)
$$F(t) = \begin{cases} 0 & t < 5 \\ \frac{1}{300}(50t - t^2 - 225) & 5 \leqslant t \leqslant 15 \\ 1 & t > 15 \end{cases}$$

(c) 0.23   (d) $m = 25 - 5\sqrt{10}$

(e) fixed start and finish unlikely

12 3

13 (a)
$$f(x) = \begin{cases} \frac{2}{5}x & 0 \leqslant x \leqslant 1 \\ \frac{2}{5} & 1 < x \leqslant 2 \\ -\frac{1}{5}x + \frac{4}{5} & 2 < x \leqslant 4 \end{cases}$$

$f(x) = 0$ otherwise

$E(X) = \frac{9}{5}$

(b) 0.125

14 (a) Po(0.25)   (c) 0.276

15 (a) 0.8692   (b) 0.0728

16 (a) $\frac{1}{6}$, $\frac{8}{9}$, $\frac{\sqrt{26}}{9}$

(b)
$$F(x) = \begin{cases} 0 & x \leqslant 0 \\ \frac{2}{3}x - \frac{x^2}{12} & 0 < x \leqslant 2 \\ 1 & x > 2 \end{cases}$$

(c) 1.354, 0.394, 0.838

(d) 0.0113

17 (a) (i) $\frac{1}{14}$ (ii) $\frac{18}{7}$ (iii) $\frac{19}{49}$

(b) (i) $\frac{1}{9}$ (ii) $\frac{9}{4}$ (iii) $\frac{27}{80}$ (iv) 2.38

18 (a) 0.2138   (b) 0.1378   (c) 0.04571

19 (a) binomial   (b) Poisson

(c) 0.013   (d) 0.014; 0.182

20 (a) Po(0.6)   (b) 0.549   (c) 0.0231

(d) The number of telephone boxes in a square kilometre is likely to be different.

21 (b) $2\frac{1}{9}$

(c)
$$F(x) = \begin{cases} 0 & x < 1 \\ \frac{1}{12}(x^2 + 2x - 3) & 1 \leqslant x < 3 \\ 1 & x \geqslant 3 \end{cases}$$

(d) 2.16

22 0.0756; 0.925; 0.4005

23 (b) 30   (c) 21.2   (d) $\frac{65}{81}$ (e) 0.039

(f) most components die quickly or fixed upper limit or high density close to zero unlikely

24 $k = \frac{3}{4} E(X) = \frac{9}{16}$, $Var(X) = \frac{107}{1280}$

(a) $P(B) = \frac{85}{256}$ (b) $P(B|A) = \frac{85}{152}$

25 (a) 0.249   (b) 0.929   (c) 0.508; 0.542

26 (a) 0.340   (b) 0.966   (c) 0.0366

(d) 0.571

27 (a) 0.991   (b) 0.983   (c) $\frac{7}{25}$

(d) 0.0017   (e) £15.40

28 (a) 0.3125   (b) 1.25   (d) $\frac{1}{16}$

(e) 1.6

(f) X – because the approximations are more reasonable

29 (a) $\frac{3}{4}$ (b) $\frac{4}{3}$ (c) $\frac{11}{16}$ (d) $\frac{6}{5}$, $\frac{4}{25}$

30 (a) 0.181   (b) 0.999   (c) 0.018

31 0.3456

32 0.8791

33 0.9940

34 (a) Probability of success (chocolate) is constant; only two outcomes.

(b) (i) 0.1623   (ii) 0.2493

35 (a) $\frac{2}{225}$

(b)
$$F(t) = \begin{cases} 0 & t \leqslant 0 \\ \frac{t^2}{225} & 0 < t \leqslant 15 \\ 1 & t > 15 \end{cases}$$

(c) $\frac{44}{225}$

36 (a) 0.864   (b) 0.301   (c) 3.67, 3.7

(d) 3.67 close to 3.71 $\Rightarrow$ Poisson

(e) 0.209

Exercise 3A

1 (a) 15, $8\frac{1}{3}$ (b) 0, 3   (c) 0.5, $\frac{3}{4}$

2 5, $\frac{4}{3}$ 0.375

3 (a) $f(x) = \frac{1}{12}$ $0 \leqslant x \leqslant 12$

(b) $\frac{1}{3}$

4 (a) $\frac{2}{3}$ (b) 120 mm, 4800 mm^2

5 $\frac{1}{3}$

6 (a) $3\frac{1}{2}$, 2.083

(b) $P(X \leqslant x_0) = \dfrac{x_0 - 1}{5}$ $1 \leqslant x_0 \leqslant 6$; 0.6

Exercise 3B

1. (a) $P(Y < 25.5)$ (b) $P(Y < 41.5)$
   (c) $P(Y > 10.5)$ (d) $P(Y > 4.5)$
   (e) $P(1.5 < Y < 9.5)$ (f) $P(40.5 < Y < 50.5)$
2. (a) $P(Y > 32.5)$ (b) $(Y < 16.5)$
   (c) $P(Y > 8.5)$ (d) $P(Y < 47.5)$
   (e) $P(23.5 < Y < 36.5)$ (f) $P(4.5 < Y < 9.5)$
3. (a), (c) and (e)
4. (a) 0.0968 (b) 0.00434 (c) 0.0724 (d) 0.223
5. (a) 0.00703 (b) 0.946 (c) 0.0401 (d) 0.7305
6. (a) 0.963 (b) 0.9596 error 0.003
7. (a) 0.821 (b) 0.825 error 0.004
8. n large, $np > 5$, $n(1 - p) > 5$
   mean $= np$, variance $= np(1 - p)$
   (a) 0.215
9. 0.0024, £13 200
10. n large, $np > 5$, $n(1 - p) > 5$
    mean $= np$, variance $= np(1 - p)$
    (b) 0.734
11. (a) 0.0590 (b) 0.825 (c) 0.311
12. (a) $0.00725 \times 100 = 1$ day
    (b) $0.0448 \times 100 = 4$ days
    (c) $0.0778 \times 100 = 8$ days
13. (a) 0.185 (b) 0.858 (c) 0.946

Exercise 4A

1. (a) infinite (b) countably infinite (c) finite
2. (a) a book (b) a car (c) a patient
3. (a) a register of all students at the university
   (b) all L-registered cars recorded at the Driver
       and Vehicle Licensing Centre, Swansea
   (c) all registered professional golfers
4. A car could be the sampling unit. Because the
   population is to all purposes infinite a
   suitable sampling frame could be all cars
   passing a check point on a given road at a
   certain time.
5. Advantages: quick, cheap, does not destroy all
   batteries
   Disadvantages: may contain natural variations
   and bias due to smallness of samples.

6. This is an infinite population so you cannot
   measure each tree. Rates of growth may vary
   in different parts of the forest – each type of
   area must be identified and an appropriate
   sampling frame drawn up. Sampling units
   must be free from bias, etc.

Exercise 4B

1. (a) Yes (b) Yes (c) No (d) Yes
   (e) No (f) No (g) Yes
2. (a) $B(20, 0.05)$ (b) 0.9245
   (c) 1, 0.95
3. (a) $B(20, p)$
   (b) $(1 - p)^{20} + 20(1 - p)^{19}p + 190(1 - p)^{18}p^2$
   (c) $\mu = 20p, \sigma^2 = 20p(1 - p)$
4. (a) $B(10, \frac{1}{4})$ (b) 0.4744, 0.0035
   (c) 2.5, 1.875
5. (a) $Po(1.5)$ (b) 0.5578
6. (a) $Po(0.8)$ (b) 0.0474 (c) $Po(2)$
7. (a) $\mu = 3\frac{5}{6}, \sigma^2 = 10.81$
   (b) {1,1}; {5,5}; {10,10}; {1,5}; {5,10}; {1,10}
   (c)

$\bar{X}$:	1	3	5	5.5	7.5	10
$p(\bar{x})$:	$\frac{9}{36}$	$\frac{12}{36}$	$\frac{4}{36}$	$\frac{6}{36}$	$\frac{4}{36}$	$\frac{1}{36}$

8. (a) $6\frac{1}{4}$
   (b) (5,5,5)
       (5,5,10) : (5,10,5) : (10,5,5)
       (5,10,10) : (10,5,10) : (10,10,5)
       (10,10,10)
   (c)

$\bar{X}$:	5	$\frac{20}{3}$	$\frac{25}{3}$	10
$p(\bar{x})$:	$\frac{27}{64}$	$\frac{27}{64}$	$\frac{9}{64}$	$\frac{1}{64}$

   (d)

M :	5	10
$p(m)$:	$\frac{27}{32}$	$\frac{5}{32}$

9. (a) 1
   (b) {0,0,0}; {0,0,1}; {0,0,2}; {0,1,2};
       {1,1,1}; {1,2,2}; {1,1,2}; {2,2,2};
       {0,1,1}
       {0,2,2}
   (c)

$\bar{X}$:	0	$\frac{1}{3}$	$\frac{2}{3}$	1	$\frac{4}{3}$	$\frac{5}{3}$	2
$p(\bar{x})$:	$\frac{1}{64}$	$\frac{6}{64}$	$\frac{15}{64}$	$\frac{20}{64}$	$\frac{15}{64}$	$\frac{6}{64}$	$\frac{1}{64}$

   (d)

N :	0	1	2
$p(n)$:	$\frac{10}{64}$	$\frac{44}{64}$	$\frac{10}{64}$

Exercise 4C

1 0.0781, not sig.
2 0.0464, sig.
3 0.0480, sig.
4 0.0049, sig.
5 0.2632, not sig.
6 $X \geqslant 5$, 0.0328
7 $X = 0$, 0.0388
8 $X \geqslant 8$, 0.0048
9 $X \leqslant 3$ or $X \geqslant 13$, 0.037
10 $X \geqslant 7$, 0.0024
11 0.1875, not sig., manufacturer not justified.
12 0.1154, not sig., no evidence of bias
13 $X \leqslant 6$
14 0.3813, not sig., no evidence probability is less than $\frac{1}{6}$
15 (a) $p > 0.05 \Rightarrow$ there is insufficient evidence to support Miss Smith's claim
   (b) 12
16 (a) 0.395
   (b) 0.865
17 (a) Bin $(n, 0.68)$ (b) 0.218
18 0.091, sig.

Exercise 4D

1 0.0424, sig.
2 0.0430, not sig.
3 0.1905, not sig.
4 $X \geqslant 9$
5 $X \leqslant 2$
6 $X = 0$
7 0.1321, not sig., no evidence of a decrease
8 0.124, new schedules do not appear to have increased the average number of late buses.

Review exercise 2

1 (a) 0.6517   (b) 0.8770
   (c) 0.9966   (d) 0.2706
2 (a) (i) 0.1969   (ii) 0.8202
   (b) (ii) 19   (c) Normal, 0.2148

3 Fixed number of trials, trials must be independent, trials have two outcomes, the probability of success is constant.
   (a) 0.102   (b) 279
4 0.02
5 (a) 0.4335   (b) 0.1841   (c) 0.021
   (d) $H_0 : \lambda = 4$; $H_1 : \lambda > 4$
   (e) no. of errors $\geqslant 8$; 0.0511
   (f) Do not reject H_0.
6 n large, $np > 5$, $np(1-p) > 5$; 2; 1.6; 0.12
7 (a) $H_0 : \mu = 9$; $H_1 : \mu < 9$
   (b) No. of defective items $\leqslant 4$; 0.0550
   (c) Do not reject H_0
8 $0, \frac{3}{4}$
9 λ large, mean $= \lambda$, variance $= \lambda$
   (a) 0.605   (b) 0.135; 0.238
10. 0.0093
11 (a) 1.72   (b) 0.0102
   (c) 0.1174   (d) 0.0840
12 $p(\geqslant 3 \text{ prefer Energise}) = 0.5$, not significant
13 Yes $(p = 0.0002)$
14 (b) 0.256   (c) 0.057
   (d) reduction in number of lorries pulling in
15 a, b and d continuous; c discrete
16 It is more cost effective; the test may be destructive.
17 a single leaf; all the leaves on the tree.
18 (a) 20, 12.5   (b) 25, 14.4
   (c) not very suitable
   (d) f(x) because of higher frequency near to 0
19 (a) 0.2493   (b) 0.1452
   (c) (i) 0.0074   (ii) 0.6790
20 (a) 0.0664   (b) 0.8606
   (c) 0.7201   (d) 0.4402
21 (a) a child   (b) all the children in the school
   (c) all English school children; No
22 (a) (i) 0.325   (ii) 0.221   (b) 3   (c) 0.224
23 $H_0 : \mu_1 = \mu_2$; $H_1 : \mu_1 > \mu_2$ (μ_1 is the mean speed after the highest level of weight training)
24 a and d $-$ H_0; b and c $-$ H_1.
25 b

26 $\mu_1 \neq \mu_2$ – two-tail test; $\mu_1 > \mu_2$ or $\mu_1 < \mu_2$ – one-tail test

27 (a) n large (b) mean large, i.e. $\lambda > 10$
   (c) small p and large n

28 0.2150; 0.5

29 a and d qualitative; b, c and e quantitative

30 P(3 or more fatalities) = 0.0011 when using a Po (0.2) distribution. There is significant evidence that the line requires further protection.

31 a and d are countably infinite; b is finite; c is infinite.

32 (a) 6 (b) 0.12 (c) 3.5 (d) $\frac{25}{12}$

33 $H_0 : p = 0.35$, $H_1 : p => 0.35$;
   $p(X \geqslant 10) = 0.1218$; 11

34 $H_0 : \lambda = 5$; $H_1 : \lambda < 5$; $p(X \leqslant 2 | \lambda = 5) = 0.1247$;
   Do not reject H_0; not significant.

Examination style paper S2

1 (a) A statistical process devised to describe or make predictions about the expected behaviour of a real world problem.
   (b) A sampling unit contains an element (or a collection of elements) from a population.
   (c) A sampling frame is a list of sampling elements.

2 (a) n large; p small
   (b) 0.1396

3 (a) 5 (b) $1\frac{1}{3}$ (c) 0.425

4 (a) Fixed number of balloons in a packet; constant probability of a blue balloon being produced.
   (b) (i) 0.1221 (ii) 0.2493 (iii) 0.1452

5 Events occur singly, independently and at a constant rate.
   (a) 0.939 (b) 0.469; 0.0227

6 (a)
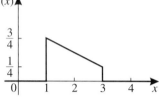

   (b) $\frac{11}{6}$; median < mean

7 (a) $H_0 : p = 0.15$; $H_1 : p < 0.15$;
   $X \sim B(20, 0.15)$;
   $P(X \leqslant 1) = 0.1756 > 0.05$; No evidence that proportion is less than 15%
   (b) Need 0, since $P(X = 0) = 0.0388$
   (c) Colours are packed randomly.
   (d) $H_0 : p = 0.15$; $H_1 : p < 0.15$;
   $Y \sim B(100, 0.15)$; $Y \cong N(15, (\sqrt{12.75})^2$;
   $P(Y \leqslant 8) = 0.0344 < 0.05$; Evidence that proportion < 15%
   (e) Individually neither would be significant, but collectively they are.

List of symbols and notation

The following notation will be used in all Edexcel examinations.

$\in$	is an element of
$\notin$	is not an element of
$\{x_1, x_2, \ldots\}$	the set with elements $x_1, x_2, \ldots$
$\{x : \ldots\}$	the set of all x such that $\ldots$
$\mathrm{n}(A)$	the number of elements in set A
$\varnothing$	the empty set
e	the universal set
A'	the complement of the set A
$\mathbb{N}$	the set of natural numbers, $\{1, 2, 3, \ldots\}$
$\mathbb{Z}$	the set of integers, $\{0, \pm 1, \pm 2, \pm 3, \ldots\}$
$\mathbb{Z}^+$	the set of positive integers, $\{1, 2, 3, \ldots\}$
$\mathbb{Z}_n$	the set of integers modulo n, $\{0, 1, 2, \ldots, n - 1\}$
$\mathbb{Q}$	the set of rational numbers $\left\{\dfrac{p}{q} : p \in \mathbb{Z}, q \in \mathbb{Z}^+\right\}$
$\mathbb{Q}^+$	the set of positive rational numbers, $\{x \in \mathbb{Q} : x > 0\}$
$\mathbb{Q}_0^+$	the set of positive rational numbers and zero, $\{x \in \mathbb{Q} : x \geqslant 0\}$
$\mathbb{R}$	the set of real numbers
$\mathbb{R}^+$	the set of positive real numbers, $\{x \in \mathbb{R} : x > 0\}$
$\mathbb{R}_0^+$	the set of positive real numbers and zero, $\{x \in \mathbb{R} : x \geqslant 0\}$
$\mathbb{C}$	the set of complex numbers
(x, y)	the ordered pair x, y
$A \times B$	the cartesian product of sets A and B, $A \times B = \{(a, b) : a \in A, b \in B\}$
$\subseteq$	is a subset of
$\subset$	is a proper subset of
$\cup$	union
$\cap$	intersection
$[a, b]$	the closed interval, $\{x \in \mathbb{R} : a \leqslant x \leqslant b\}$
$[a, b), [a, b[$	the interval $\{x \in \mathbb{R} : a \leqslant x < b\}$
$(a, b],]a, b]$	the interval $\{x \in \mathbb{R} : a < x \leqslant b\}$
$(a, b),]a, b[$	the open interval $\{x \in \mathbb{R} : a < x < b\}$
$y \, R \, x$	y is related to x by the relation R
$y \sim x$	y is equivalent to x, in the context of some equivalence relation
$=$	is equal to
$\neq$	is not equal to
$\equiv$	is identical to *or* is congruent to

$\approx$	is approximately equal to
$\cong$	is isomorphic to
$\propto$	is proportinal to
$<$	is less than
$\leqslant$, $\not>$	is less than or equal to, is not greater than
$>$	is greater than
$\geqslant$, $\not<$	is greater than or equal to, is not less than
∞	infinity
$p \wedge q$	p and q
$p \vee q$	p or q (or both)
$\sim p$	not p
$p \Rightarrow q$	p implies q (if p then q)
$p \Leftarrow q$	p is implied by q (if q then p)
$p \Leftrightarrow q$	p implies and is implied by q (p is equivalent to q)
$\exists$	there exists
$\forall$	for all
$a + b$	a plus b
$a - b$	a minus b
$a \times b$, ab, $a.b$	a multiplied by b
$a \div b$, $\dfrac{a}{b}$, a/b	a divided by b
$\displaystyle\sum_{i=1}^{n} a_i$	$a_1 + a_2 + \ldots + a_n$
$\displaystyle\prod_{i=1}^{n} a_i$	$a_1 \times a_2 \times \ldots \times a_n$
$\sqrt{a}$	the positive square root of a
$|a|$	the modulus of a
$n!$	n factorial
$\dbinom{n}{r}$	the binomial coefficient $\dfrac{n!}{r!(n-r)!}$ for $n \in \mathbb{Z}^{+}$ $\dfrac{n(n-1)\ldots(n-r+1)}{r!}$ for $n \in \mathbb{Q}$
$f(x)$	the value of the function f at x
$f : A \to B$	f is a function under which each element of set A has an image in set B
$f : x \mapsto y$	the function f maps the element x to the element y
f^{-1}	the inverse function of the function f
$g \circ f$, gf	the composite function of f and g which is defined by $(g \circ f)(x)$ or $gf(x) = g(f(x))$
$\displaystyle\lim_{x \to a} f(x)$	the limit of f(x) as x tends to a
Δx, δx	an increment of x
$\dfrac{dy}{dx}$	the derivative of y with respect to x
$\dfrac{d^n y}{dx^n}$	the nth derivative of y with respect to x

$f'(x), f''(x), \ldots f^{(n)}(x)$	the first, second, ... nth derivatives of $f(x)$ with respect to x
$\displaystyle\int y \, dx$	the indefinite integral of y with respect to x
$\displaystyle\int_a^b y \, dx$	the definite integral of y with respect to x betweent he limits $x = a$ and $x = b$
$\dfrac{\partial V}{\partial x}$	the partial derivative of V with respect to x
$\dot{x}, \ddot{x}, \ldots$	the first, second, . . . derivatives of x with respect to t
e	base of natural logarithms
e^x, exp x	exponential function of x
$\log_a x$	logarithm to the base a of x
$\ln x$, $\log_e x$	natural logarithm of x
$\lg x$, $\log_{10} x$	logarithm of x to base 10
sin, cos, tan cosec, sec, cot	the circular functions
arcsin, arccos, arctan arccosec, arcsec, arccot	the inverse circular functions
sinh, cosh, tanh cosech, sech, coth	the hyperbolic functions
arsinh, arcosh, artanh, arcosech, arsech, arcoth	the inverse hyperbolic functions
i, j	square root of -1
z	a complex number, $z = x + iy$
Re z	the real part of z, Re $z = x$
Im z	the imaginary part of z, Im $z = y$
$|z|$	the modulus of z, $|z| = \sqrt{(x^2 + y^2)}$
arg z	the argument of z, arg $z = \arctan\dfrac{y}{x}$
z^*	the complex conjugate of z, $x - iy$
$\mathbf{M}$	a matrix $\mathbf{M}$
$\mathbf{M}^{-1}$	the inverse of the matrix $\mathbf{M}$
$\mathbf{M}^{\mathrm{T}}$	the transpose of the matrix $\mathbf{M}$
det $\mathbf{M}$, $|\mathbf{M}|$	the determinant of the square matrix $\mathbf{M}$
$\mathbf{a}$	the vector $\mathbf{a}$
$\overrightarrow{AB}$	the vector represented in magnitude and direction by the directed line segment AB
$\hat{\mathbf{a}}$	a unit vector in the direction of $\mathbf{a}$
$\mathbf{i}, \mathbf{j}, \mathbf{k}$	unit vectors in the directions of the cartesian coordinate axes
$|\mathbf{a}|$, a	the magnitude of $\mathbf{a}$
$|\overrightarrow{AB}|$, AB	the magnitude of $\overrightarrow{AB}$
$\mathbf{a} . \mathbf{b}$	the scalar product of $\mathbf{a}$ and $\mathbf{b}$
$\mathbf{a} \times \mathbf{b}$	the vector product of $\mathbf{a}$ and $\mathbf{b}$

A, B, C, etc	events
$A \cup B$	union of the events A and B
$A \cap B$	intersection of the events A and B
$P(A)$	probability of the event A
A'	complement of the event A
$P(A\|B)$	probability of the event A conditional on the event B
X, Y, R, etc.	random variables
x, y, r, etc.	values of the random variables X, Y, R, etc
$x_1, x_2 \ldots$	observations
$f_1, f_2, \ldots$	frequencies with which the observations $x_1, x_2, \ldots$ occur
$p(x)$	probability function $P(X = x)$ of the discrete random variable X
$p_1, p_2, \ldots$	probabilities of the values $x_1, x_2, \ldots$ of the discrete random variable X
$f(x), g(x), \ldots$	the value of the probability density function of a continuous random variable X
$F(x), G(x), \ldots$	the value of the (cumulative) distribution function $P(X \leqslant x)$ of a continuous random variable X
$E(X)$	expectation of the random variable X
$E[g(X)]$	expectation of $g(X)$
$Var(X)$	variance of the random variable X
$G(t)$	probability generating function for a random variable which takes the values $0, 1, 2, \ldots$
$B(n, p)$	binomial distribution with parameters n and p
$N(\mu, \sigma^2)$	normal distribution with mean μ and variance σ^2
μ	population mean
σ^2	population variance
σ	population standard deviation
$\bar{x}, m$	sample mean
$s^2, \hat{\sigma}^2$	unbiased estimate of population variance from a sample, $$s^2 = \frac{1}{n-1}\sum(x_i - \bar{x})^2$$
ϕ	probability density function of the standardised normal variable with distribution $N(0, 1)$
Φ	corresponding cumulative distribution function
ρ	product-moment correlation coefficient for a population
r	product-moment correlation coefficient for a sample
$Cov(X, Y)$	covariance of X and Y

Index